THE
STUDENT'S
GUIDE TO
The Bible

THE STUDENT'S GUIDE TO
The Bible

PHILIP YANCEY
TIM STAFFORD

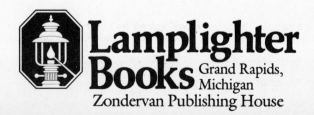
Lamplighter Books Grand Rapids, Michigan
Zondervan Publishing House

The Student's Guide to the Bible
Copyright © 1988, 1986, 1982 The Zondervan Corporation
All Rights Reserved

Lamplighter Books are published by the Zondervan Publishing House
1415 Lake Drive, S.E., Grand Rapids, Michigan 49506

Library of Congress Cataloging in Publication Data

Yancey, Philip.
    The student's guide to the Bible.

    "Based on The student Bible"—Introd.
    1. Bible—Introductions. I. Stafford, Tim.
II. Bible. English. New International. 1986. III. Title.
BS475.2.Y37 1988   220.6'1   88-23080
ISBN 0-310-58961-4

Printed in the United States of America

88 89 90 91 92 93 / DH / 10 9 8 7 6 5 4 3 2 1

Contents

Introduction

This guide is based on *The Student Bible;* all its materials are taken from that edition of the New International Version of the Bible. *The Student's Guide,* like *The Student Bible,* is aimed to help those who are relatively new at Bible reading, or who feel they need some extra orientation.

Those who already own *The Student Bible* won't need this guide. However, many people already have a Bible they're attached to or prefer a translation other than the NIV. *The Student's Guide to the Bible* will enable them to profit from some of the help offered by *The Student Bible.*

We mean these pages not as a separate book that explains all about the Bible, but as a guidebook to carry along with you as you read the Bible for yourself. A guidebook tells you where to start looking and helps you to understand what you're looking at. It doesn't look for you.

Why Do So Many Fail?

The Bible is the most wonderful, life-giving book ever written. Every Christian knows that. And contrary to some who act as though reading your Bible is the moral equivalent of eating your broccoli, most Christians would like to read their Bibles. They believe it would do them good if they did.

Yet unfortunately, a great many people who would like to read the Bible, who would like to know what it says, and who would like to use it on a daily basis, fail to do so. Why? Something more than mere laziness is involved.

"Something More"

In preparing to work on *The Student Bible,* that "something more" was impressed on us repeatedly. Both of us have been reading the Bible more or less regularly since we were children. The last few years have given us unusual opportunities to study the Bible in depth. One result of such an experience has been a deepening appreciation for the richness of the Bible. However, another result of our study has been a deepening appreciation for how difficult some parts of the Bible can be to understand.

After all, most of the Bible was written thousands of years ago. For many people, the next oldest literature they've ever read is Shakespeare—which is roughly one-tenth as old. Most people need some special notes to understand Shakespeare because the language and the culture have changed. It's no wonder they come away from some parts of the Bible unsure of what they've read.

What's more, the Bible is written by dozens of different authors in many different styles. The Book of Proverbs and the Book of Revelation could hardly be more unlike one another!

They Leave Out Half of God's Word

The result of language, cultural, and style barriers in the Bible is that many people settle for reading the fairly narrow band of its books they find easier to understand. Typically, they can relate to Psalms (at least some of the psalms), Romans, Matthew, John, Acts, Ephesians, and Philippians. Perhaps a handful of other books make their list. But they leave out at least half of God's inspired Word. They know there's an Ezekiel back there, but they never read it. Without some help, they quite possibly never will.

An even worse result is that some people—a lot of people, actually—seldom read the Bible at all. They just "don't get around to it." They have good feelings about the Bible (and some guilt feelings when they hear others talk about their "daily devotions"), but they've never been able to develop a regular pattern of Bible reading. When they try, they soon get discouraged. They can't always make the connection between what they're reading and their own lives.

The Student's Guide to the Bible is meant to help. It contains an introduction to each book in the entire Bible. These introductions are written in readable magazine style. They try to relate each book to life as we experience it. They also give some suggestions on "How to Read This Book"—since the varied literature of the Bible can't all be approached in exactly the same way. Of course these introductions don't explain every difficult point in the Bible; you'd need detailed commentaries for that. We hope, though, that they give just enough orientation so that you'll understand what each book is talking about, how it fits into the whole Bible, and how you can relate it to your life.

Nobody can read the Bible for you. Commitment and discipline are required. We hope, however, that the *Student's Guide,* like its parent *The Student Bible,* will help many people turn good intentions into good results. We believe that the Bible is God's Word. Believing that, we believe that it must be God's intention for us to read and understand it.

—Philip Yancey and Tim Stafford

Overview:
The Old Testament

The Five Books

The first five books of the Bible tell the origins of the Jewish race and culture.

GENESIS: The book of beginnings describes creation, the first rebellions against God, and God's choosing of Abraham and his offspring.

EXODUS: God rescued the Israelites from slavery in Egypt and led them to the Sinai Desert. There, he gave Moses the laws to govern the new nation.

LEVITICUS: God set up laws for the Israelites, mostly regarding holiness and worship.

NUMBERS: Because of their rebellion and disobedience, the Israelites had to wander in a wilderness for 40 years before entering the promised land.

DEUTERONOMY: Just before his death, Moses made three emotional farewell speeches, recapping history and warning the Israelites against further mistakes.

History Books

The next 12 books continue the history of the Israelites: they moved into the land of Canaan and established a kingdom that lasted almost 500 years.

JOSHUA: After Moses' death, Joshua commanded the armies that conquered much of the territory in the promised land.

JUDGES: The new nation fell into a series of dismal failures. God raised up leaders called "judges."

RUTH: This story of love and loyalty between two widows shines out brightly in an otherwise dark period.

1 SAMUEL: Samuel became a transition leader between the time of the judges and that of the kings. He appointed Israel's first king, Saul. After his own failure, Saul tried violently to prevent God's king-elect David from taking the throne.

2 SAMUEL: David, "a man after God's own heart," brought the nation together. But after committing adultery and murder, he was haunted by family and national crises.

1 KINGS: Solomon succeeded David, with mixed success. At his death, a civil war tore apart the nation. Successive kings were mostly bad, and the prophet Elijah had dramatic confrontations with King Ahab.

2 KINGS: This book continues the record of the rulers of the divided kingdom. None of the Northern kings followed God consistently, and so Israel was finally destroyed by an invader. The South, Judah, lasted much longer, but finally Babylon conquered Judah and deported its citizens.

1 CHRONICLES: The book opens with the most complete genealogical record in the Bible, then adds many incidents from the life of David (often the same as those in 2 Samuel).

2 CHRONICLES: Often paralleling the books of Kings, this book records the history of the rulers of Judah, emphasizing the good kings.

EZRA: After being held captive in Babylon for decades, the Jews were allowed to return to their homeland. Ezra, a priest, emerged from one of the first waves of refugees.

NEHEMIAH: Nehemiah returned from the Babylonian captivity after the temple had been rebuilt. He concentrated on restoring the protective wall around Jerusalem and joined Ezra in leading a religious revival.

ESTHER: This story is set among captive Jews in Persia. A courageous Jewish queen foiled a plan to exterminate her people.

Books of Poetry

Almost one-third of the Old Testament was originally written in poetry. These books concentrate on questions about pain, God, life, and love.

JOB: The best man of his day suffered the greatest personal tragedy. The entire book deals with the question, "Why?"

PSALMS: These prayers and hymns cover the full range of human emotion; together, they represent a personal journal of how to relate to God. Some were also used in public worship services.

PROVERBS: The proverbs offer advice on every imaginable area of life. The style of wise living described here leads to a fulfilled life.

ECCLESIASTES: A life without God, "under the sun," leads to meaninglessness and despair, says the Teacher in a strikingly modern book.

SONG OF SONGS: This beautiful poem celebrates romantic and physical love.

Books of the Prophets

During the years when kings ruled Israel and Judah, God spoke through prophets. Though some prophets did predict future events, their primary role was to call God's people back to him.

ISAIAH: The most eloquent of the prophets, Isaiah analyzed the failures of all the nations around him and pointed to a future Messiah who would bring peace.

JEREMIAH: Jeremiah led an emotionally tortured life, yet held to his stern message. He spoke to Judah in the last decades before Babylon destroyed the nation.

LAMENTATIONS: All Jeremiah's warnings about Jerusalem came true, and Lamentations records five poems of sorrow for the fallen city.

EZEKIEL: Ezekiel spoke to the Jews who were captive in Babylon. He often used dramatic stories and "enacted parables" to make his points.

DANIEL: A captive in Babylon, Daniel rose to the office of prime minister. Despite intense political pressure, he lived a model life of integrity and left highly symbolic prophecies about the future.

HOSEA: By marrying a loose-living wife, Hosea lived out his message: that Israel had committed spiritual adultery against God.

JOEL: Beginning with a recent catastrophe in Judah (a locust plague), Joel foretold God's judgment on Judah.

AMOS: A country boy, Amos preached to Israel at the height of its prosperity. His grim warnings focused on materialism.

OBADIAH: Obadiah warned Edom, a nation bordering Judah.

JONAH: Jonah reluctantly went to Nineveh and found Israel's enemies responsive to God's message.

MICAH: Micah exposed corruption in every level of society, but closed with a promise of forgiveness and restoration.

NAHUM: Long after Jonah had stirred Nineveh to repentance, Nahum foretold the mighty city's total destruction.

HABAKKUK: Habakkuk addressed his book to God, not people. In a frank dialogue with God, he discussed problems of suffering and justice.

ZEPHANIAH: Zephaniah focused on the coming day of the Lord, which would purge Judah, resulting in a remnant used to bless the entire world.

HAGGAI: After returning from the Babylonian captivity, the Jews began rebuilding the temple of God. But before long they set aside that task to work on their own homes. Haggai reminded them to put God first.

ZECHARIAH: Writing around the same time as Haggai, Zechariah also urged the Jews to work on the temple. He used a more uplifting approach, describing how the temple would point to the coming Messiah.

MALACHI: The last Old Testament prophet, Malachi faced a nation that had grown indifferent. He sought to stir them from apathy.

Overview: The New Testament

History Books

The word *gospel* means "good news." Almost half the New Testament consists of four accounts of the life of Jesus and the good news he brought to earth. Each of these four books, or Gospels, has a different focus and a different audience; taken together, they give a complete picture of Jesus' life and teaching. About a third of their pages are devoted to the events of his last week on earth, including the crucifixion and resurrection.

Acts continues the history into the period after Jesus left earth.

MATTHEW: Written to a Jewish audience, this Gospel links the Old and New Testaments. It presents Jesus as the Messiah and King promised in the Old Testament. Matthew emphasizes Jesus' authority and power.

MARK: Mark probably had pragmatic Roman readers in mind. His Gospel stresses action and gives a straightforward, blow-by-blow account of Jesus' work on earth.

LUKE: A doctor, Luke was also a fine writer. His Gospel provides many details of human interest, especially in Jesus' treatment of the poor and needy. A joyful tone characterizes Luke's book.

JOHN: John has a different, more reflective style than the other Gospels. Its author selected seven signs that point to Jesus as the Son of God and wove together everything else to underscore that point.

ACTS: Acts tells what happened to Jesus' followers after he left them. Peter and Paul soon emerged as leaders of the rapidly spreading church.

The Letters

The young church was nourished by apostles who set down their beliefs and messages in a series of letters. The first 13 such letters (Romans through Philemon) were written by the apostle Paul, who led the advance of Christianity to non-Jewish people.

Paul's Letters:

ROMANS: Written for a sophisticated audience, Romans sets forth theology in a logical, organized form.

1 CORINTHIANS: A very practical book, 1 Corinthians takes up the problems of a tumultuous church in Corinth: marriage, factions, immorality, public worship, and lawsuits.

2 CORINTHIANS: Paul wrote this follow-up letter to defend himself against a rebellion led by certain false apostles.

GALATIANS: A short version of the message of Romans, this book addresses legalism. It shows how Christ came to bring freedom, not bondage to a set of laws.

EPHESIANS: Although written in jail, this letter is Paul's most optimistic and encouraging. It tells of the advantages a believer has in Christ.

PHILIPPIANS: The church at Philippi ranked among Paul's favorites. This friendly letter stresses that joy can be found in any situation.

COLOSSIANS: Written to oppose certain cults, Colossians tells how faith in Christ is complete. Nothing needs to be added to what Christ did.

1 THESSALONIANS: Composed early in Paul's ministry, this letter gives a capsule history of one church, as well as Paul's direct advice about specific problems.

2 THESSALONIANS: Stronger in tone than his first letter to the Thessalonians, the sequel goes over the same topics, especially the church's questions about Christ's second coming.

1 TIMOTHY: As Paul neared the end of his life, he chose young men such as Timothy to carry on his work. His two letters to Timothy form a leadership manual for a young pastor.

2 TIMOTHY: Written just before Paul's death, 2 Timothy offers Paul's final words to his young assistant.

TITUS: Titus was left in Crete, a notoriously difficult place to nurture a church. Paul's letter gave practical advice on how to go about it.

PHILEMON: Paul urged Philemon, owner of runaway slave Onesimus, to forgive his slave and accept him as a brother in Christ.

Other Letters:

HEBREWS: No one knows who wrote Hebrews, but it probably first went to Christians in danger of slipping back into Judaism. It interprets the Old Testament, explaining many Jewish practices as symbols that prepared the way for Christ.

JAMES: James, a man of action, emphasized the right kind of behavior for a believer. Someone who calls himself a Christian ought to act like it, James believed, and his letter spells out the specifics.

1 PETER: Early Christians often met violent opposition, and Peter's letter comforted and encouraged Christians who were being persecuted for their faith.

2 PETER: In contrast to Peter's first letter, this one focused on problems that sprang up from the inside. It warns against false teachers.

1 JOHN: John could fill simple words—*light, love, life*—with deep meaning, and in this letter, he elegantly explains basic truths about the Christian life.

2 JOHN: Warning against false teachers, John counseled churches on how to respond to them.

3 JOHN: Balancing 2 John, this companion letter mentions the need to be hospitable to true teachers.

JUDE: Jude gave a brief but fiery exposé of heretics.

REVELATION: A book of visions and symbols, Revelation is the only New Testament book that concentrates on prophecy. It completes the story, begun in Genesis, of the cosmic battle between good and evil being waged on earth. It ends with a picture of a new heaven and new earth.

GENESIS

INTRODUCTION

God at Work

Everything—literally everything—begins here

The Bible begins with words that have become famous, "In the beginning God created." God, like an artist, fashioned a universe. How can we grasp the grandeur of this?

Michelangelo, perhaps the greatest artist in history, may help us to understand. He painted the famous Sistine Chapel to retell Genesis' story of creation. His experience proves one thing: creativity is work.

An Exhausting Effort

Michelangelo had 6,000 square feet of ceiling to cover—the size of four average house roofs. Anyone who has painted a ceiling with a roller has caught a hint of the physical difficulty of such a task. But Michelangelo's plan called for 300 separate, detailed portraits of men and women. For more than three years the 5'4" artist devoted all his labors to the exhausting strain of painting the vast overhead space with his tiny brushes.

Sometimes he painted standing on a huge scaffold, a paintbrush high over his head. Sometimes he sat, his nose inches from the ceiling. Sometimes he painted while lying on his back. His back, shoulders, neck, and arms cramped painfully.

In the long days of summer, he had light to paint 17 hours a day, taking food and a chamberpot with him on the 60-foot scaffold. For 30 days at a stretch he slept in his clothes, not even taking off his boots. Paint dribbled into his eyes so he could barely see. Freezing in the winter, sweating in the summer, he painted until at last the ceiling looked like a ceiling no more. He had transformed it into the creation drama, with creatures so real they seemed to breathe. Never before or since have paint and plaster been so changed.

The Miracle of Life

But, as Michelangelo knew very well, his work was a poor, dim image of what God had created. Over the plaster vault of the Sistine Chapel rose the immense dome of God's sky, breathtaking in its simple beauty. Mountains, seas, the continents—all these, and much more, are the creative work of God, the master artist.

God's world, so much bigger and more beautiful than Michelangelo's masterpiece, is the product of incomparably greater energy. As Eugene Peterson has written, "The Bible begins with the announcement, 'In the beginning God created' not 'sat majestic in the heavens,' and not 'was filled with beauty and love.' He created. He did something." In the beginning, God went to work.

Genesis focuses attention on this creative, hard-working God. The word *God* appears 30 times in the 31 verses of chapter 1. He grabs our attention in action. Genesis is an account of his deeds, ringing splendidly with the magnificent effort of creation.

Mending Broken Pieces

Genesis also talks about the work of humankind—but the tone changes abruptly. God had barely finished creating the universe when human rebellion marred it, like a delinquent spraying graffiti on the Sistine Chapel. Chapters 3-11 of Genesis portray a series of disasters: Adam and Eve's rebellion, Cain's calculated murder of his brother, the worldwide wickedness leading to the great flood, and human arrogance at Babel.

God immediately began to mend the pieces his creatures had broken. He narrowed his scope from the whole universe to a single man—not a king or wealthy landowner, but a childless nomad, Abraham. Abraham, Sarah, Isaac, Rebekah, Jacob, Rachel, Joseph—the upward thrust from chapter 12 on came through God's work in these startlingly human individuals. They were far from perfect, yet God picked them up where they were and carried them forward. He promised them great things. He moved through them to restore his art. His creative activity did not stop on the seventh day.

Genesis and Revelation

Many people read the Old Testament as though it portrayed the "bad old days" before Jesus. But that's not an accurate picture. Actually, the first three chapters of Genesis link to the last book of the Bible, Revelation. They are like brackets of perfection around the sadness of life marred by sin, death, suffering, and hatred. In Genesis we learn that life didn't start out that way. In Revelation we find out it won't end that way either. But the Old and New Testaments take place between those brackets. Through Abraham, through Moses, ultimately in Jesus, God is hard at work to make things right.

How to Read Genesis

Genesis is one of the most enjoyable Old Testament books, full of memorable stories of people and events. It is a crucial book to know, for the rest of the Bible often refers back to it.

Genesis tells the story of many beginnings—the beginning of the universe, the beginning of sin, and perhaps most important, the beginning of God's work to restore a sinful humanity.

The book breaks into two major sections. The first 11 chapters take a big view. They give the origins of human society, including the familiar stories of Adam and Eve, Cain and Abel, Noah's ark, and the tower of Babel. Here, a few words carry great significance. You need to read slowly and reflectively, for what happens in a single line may echo off events for centuries to come. For instance, Adam and Eve's sin, because it was the *first* sin, became an emblem of disobedience against God.

Beginning at chapter 12, Genesis tells a different kind of story—that of a single family. The pace of the story slows to develop the personalities of Abraham, Isaac, Jacob, and Joseph. These fathers and sons are full of human faults and oddities. Do you recognize any of their traits in people you know?

Seeing their fully human personalities, try to understand what God's plans were for them as individuals—and through them, for the restoration of a whole world marred by sin.

Notes

_____

_____

_____

_____

_____

EXODUS

INTRODUCTION

Free at Last

The slaves in Egypt get a liberator

Nothing stirs a nation's blood like a liberator. The United States remembers two especially: Washington and Lincoln. George Washington led the original fight for independence. A century later Abraham Lincoln set three million people free. For those slaves, Lincoln was a true liberator.

Other places, too, have liberators. India called a scrawny little man named Gandhi "Mahatma" (or "the great one") for leading his people to freedom. South America memorializes Simon Bolivar. For the Jews, one liberator named Moses accomplished what all these did—and more.

The Bible devotes one-eighth of its pages to the story of Moses' time (a bulk of material two-thirds the length of the entire New Testament). And when Jesus came as the great Liberator who set all humanity free, the New Testament reached back to Moses for a comparison (Hebrews 3:1-6).

Bondage in Egypt

The time was ripe for a liberator. Genesis closed with Jacob's family of 70 moving to Egypt. But in the opening scene of Exodus, 350 years later, hundreds of thousands of their ancestors were toiling on Pharaoh's huge construction projects—not as guests but as slaves.

One particularly ruthless pharaoh ordered the murder of all male Jewish babies, unwittingly setting the stage for one of the great ironies of history. Moses' parents hid him in a watertight basket among the grasses of a swamp. There, the tiny baby caught the eye of the pharaoh's daughter. The very edict intended to destroy the Jews led to their deliverance.

Adopted into the palace, Moses got the benefit of a superb classical education. His Egyptian upbringing was balanced by Jewish nurture: in another striking irony, the pharaoh's daughter paid Moses' own mother to nurse him. The son of slaves, yet brought up in the seat of power, Moses prepared for his eventual goal of forging a nation out of a ragtag band of captives.

His career had to wait, though, for a period of humbling in the desert. Moses fled Egypt as a brash, self-confident man who liked to take matters into his own hands. Forty years later he reluctantly returned, with little besides a stick and a donkey.

Free at Last

The Jews had endured nearly four centuries of oppression—twice as long as the history of America as a nation—before liberation. So far as we know, during those years they received no direct communication from heaven. Surely God must have seemed silent.

Moses faced a formidable challenge. Somehow he had to earn the trust of the slaves and inspire hope in them so that they could indeed throw off their chains. He had to prove that God had not forgotten them. When the time was right, God unleashed a spectacle of might and power that brought a cruel pharaoh to his knees—and convinced the Israelites that God really did care for them.

God used Moses in remarkable ways. He was the first person recorded in the Bible to work miracles. He met God in intimate ways granted no other human. He had a hand in the authorship of a good portion of the Old Testament. But in Jewish history he earned a place primarily as a liberator. He led the march from slavery to freedom, from Egypt to the promised land.

How to Read Exodus

Exodus divides neatly into two parts. The first 20 chapters, on the Jews' flight from Egypt, read like an exciting novel. Movies based on the action here have strained Hollywood special-effects crews. Everything else in the Old Testament flows out of the events of the exodus—these 20 chapters simply cannot be missed.

As you read Exodus, look for important lessons that apply to your life. For example, study the life of Moses, one of a handful of truly great leaders in history. Chapter 18 shows Moses learning an important leadership principle, and chapters 32-35 include encounters and conversations with God that have no equal in the Bible.

Exodus contains much material about the nature of God. Search for each place where God makes an appearance. Exodus shows a greater proportion of miracles—direct supernatural acts of God—than any part of the Bible except the Gospels. Why were these miracles done? Can you see a pattern? What should the Israelites have learned from them? Did they?

The last 20 chapters mainly consist of laws and regulations, given at Mount Sinai, to govern the life of the nation. Read them to note the concerns and priorities important to God as he designs an entire culture.

The instructions are usually clustered in groups, encompassing every area of life:
1. Moral rules, such as the Ten Commandments
2. Civil and social rules, much like a criminal code
3. Religious and ceremonial rules for the Jews.

The religious rituals with their many sacrifices and festivals seem strange to modern Westerners, but they were not at all unusual then. Also, they prepared the way for a Redeemer who was greater than Moses: Jesus Christ. You will need study books and commentaries to find all the symbols that apply to Jesus' life, as shown, for example, in the Passover. Fortunately, the Bible includes a brief but powerful commentary in Hebrews (see especially Hebrews 7-10.). This book should be read alongside Exodus and the three books that follow.

Notes

_____

_____

_____

_____

_____

LEVITICUS

INTRODUCTION

Living with Fire

Dangerous material more powerful than the atom

Leviticus seems mighty strange to the modern world. Unlike most of the Bible, it has few personalities and stories, and no poetry. Instead, it is crammed full of detailed rules and procedures.

Its painstaking ritual is, however, strikingly similar to the procedures surrounding nuclear technology. The specialized clothing, the concern for purification, the precise handling of crucial materials—both nuclear workers and Old Testament priests share these. This similarity gives an important clue to understanding Leviticus.

Cleaning Up a Nuclear Spill

At the Hanford plutonium separation plant in eastern Washington, plutonium and U-235 are kept in a special high-security vault, in brass cans wrapped three times in plastic. To move the radioactive material, specially trained handlers don white protection overalls and special breather masks. They never touch the materials except through a sealed "glove box."

If an accident occurs, such as a small fire ignited by the "hot" material, the entire area must be cleansed through laborious scrubbing with soap and water. Carefully trained workers dispose of the dirty water in a specially protected toxic waste area. Anyone contaminated must be similarly "cleansed" from the exposure. In extreme cases, she or he must stay away from other people for months.

These rigid rules grew from hard experience. For decades no one knew the dangers of radioactivity. Workers who used radioactive materials to hand-paint the first "glow in the dark" watches licked their paintbrushes to get a fine tip; their supervisors said they would gain sex appeal. Instead, they got cancer. The introduction of nuclear weapons and nuclear power plants increased the amount of radioactive material being handled. Gradually scientists realized: if you are going to use the atom, you must adopt procedures to fit its power.

The Intimate Presence of God

Leviticus reads something like a training manual for atomic plant workers. Its "dangerous material," however, is more powerful than the atom. Leviticus gives exhaustive detail on how to live with God.

A pamphlet on "how to survive a nuclear accident" may be dull if read on vacation, but it's gripping if read in a vibrating nuclear reactor. Similarly, Leviticus is dull if you do not realize the wonderful news behind it: a powerful God, the creator of the universe, has entered the life of a small and insignificant tribe. The Israelites could not merely fit this God into their lives. They needed to restructure their lives—food, sex, economics—to fit with his. It was essential not just for priests, but for everyone.

Ignoring the operations manual could be deadly. It was for Aaron's two sons (chapter 10).

Free from Contamination

Today, because of Jesus Christ, we don't live in the world of Leviticus. Jesus' perfect self-sacrifice made the daily sacrifice of animals unnecessary. He replaced the high priest as our representative before God. Jesus cleanses the real source of contamination, our sinful nature. Leviticus was meant to teach people some basic truths about God, and when their lessons were complete, they could go on to bigger and better things. (The New Testament book of Hebrews spells out this graduation.)

Yet we need to be reminded of the principles Leviticus taught. It tells us that God was then, as he is today, "a consuming fire" (Hebrews 12:29). He has taught us how to live with that fire, not because we deserved to know, but because he wanted our company. We dare not treat him lightly.

How to Read Leviticus

Many well-intentioned readers, determined to read the Bible from beginning to end, bog down in Leviticus. It's a law book, a procedural manual for getting along with a holy and powerful God. Sheer detail can bore you, especially if you miss the point behind it.

When you read the Bible, careful attention to detail is usually a key to understanding. In Leviticus, however, you will get more from looking at the big picture than from studying the details. Some laws we simply don't understand. But Leviticus as a whole shows what kind of people God wanted Israel to be. As you read, keep your mind on the big picture.

Notes

_____

_____

_____

_____

_____

NUMBERS

INTRODUCTION

Forty Years of Misery

A joyous adventure comes to a tragic end

As Numbers opens, the Israelites are gearing up for a great adventure. Free at last from the chains of slavery, they are headed for the promised land. Yet the book that begins with a bang ends with a whimper. Weeks, months, and then years in a hostile desert have seemed to melt the spirit of adventure. The Israelites act like people who have lost their moorings. In relentness detail, Numbers records a whole sequence of grumblings and rebellions.

Forty-Year Detour

Stomachs complained first, as the Israelites began to long for the spices of Egypt. Soon, the great mob of people simply unraveled. At least ten times they lashed out in despair or rose up in open rebellion. They plotted against their leaders and denounced God. Revolt spread to the priests, to the top military scouts, to Moses' family, and finally to Moses himself.

The original Hebrew title of this book was not "Numbers" but rather "In the desert," and this cryptic phrase expresses a little of the Israelites' futility. Surrounded by hostile nations, they had to march under the broiling sun in a desert plagued by snakes, scorpions, and drought. Even today, visitors to the Sinai Desert marvel that an entire nation wandered that ground for so long.

A march through the desert should have taken about two weeks. Instead, it took almost 40 years. Numbers spans the years of wandering and ends where the trek began: at the very spot (Kadesh) where the Israelites' faith had failed. Of the many thousands who left Egypt, only two adults, Joshua and Caleb, would make it into the promised land.

A Different Kind of History

Most ancient histories sound very different from this book. They tell of heroic exploits by mighty warriors and unblemished leaders. With an almost numbing monotony, Numbers presents a far more realistic picture. It shows the early symptoms, the full progression, and the tragic end of grumbling and unbelief.

The Israelites lost faith not only in themselves, but in their God. Because of that, a whole generation of them lies buried in the peninsula known as Sinai.

References to the "desert wanderings" crop up again and again in the Bible. The period of rebellion left an indelible mark on the Jewish people. Exactly what went wrong? The book of Numbers is given to tell us. The apostle Paul points out that these failures "happened to them as examples and were written down as warnings for us, on whom the fulfillment of the ages has come. So, if you think you are standing firm, be careful that you don't fall!" (1 Corinthians 10:11-12).

How to Read Numbers

People who read straight through Numbers very often come away confused or discouraged. The book begins with a long description of a census and proceeds into lists of laws and rituals. These were the official records of a nation, and each word had great significance for the Israelites. (Imagine how our Yellow Pages or Congressional Record would appear to people 3,000 years from now.)

Yet, unlike Leviticus, Numbers does not consist mainly of these long descriptions. Rather, it focuses on stories, with laws and rituals sprinkled in at various points. The stories are exciting, and some, such as the story of Balaam, are quite remarkable.

The action in Numbers takes place in three different settings: (1) Chapters 1-14 begin in the same place Exodus ended: at the foot of Mount Sinai. (2) Chapters 15-19 cover a period of 37 years, the time of the desert wanderings. Moses' summary in chapter 33 lists 42 stops in the wilderness, but Numbers details very few of them. (3) Chapters 20-36 concern a whole new generation of Israelites, who were making final preparations before the invasion.

As you read Numbers, it will help to have a major theme in mind, such as grumbling and rebellion. Work through the book, looking at examples of this problem. Major outbreaks occur in chapters 11, 12, 13, 14, 16, 20, and 21—at least ten incidents in all. Notice the cause of each rebellion, and also God's response. Can you see parallels to the Israelites' experience in your own life?

Numbers also offers insight into the leadership of Moses by showing his response to each crisis. One illustration of his prominence: over 80 times the book says that "the LORD said to Moses." Look for the qualities, both positive and negative, that made him an effective leader.

Other parts of the Bible often refer to Numbers. Some of the historical psalms, such as Psalms 78, 105, and 136, recast these events in poetry.

Notes

_____

_____

_____

_____

_____

DEUTERONOMY

INTRODUCTION

A Personal Plea

Moses' last chance with the people he loved

Politicians get this advice: "When you deliver a speech, make it seem as if you're having a personal talk in a small room with each one of your listeners." No one took that advice better than Franklin Delano Roosevelt—unless, perhaps, you consider Moses' speeches in Deuteronomy.

When Roosevelt became president of the United States in 1932, he faced a national crisis greater than any since the Civil War. Fifteen million people were unemployed in the Great Depression, and two million of those wandered around the country, homeless, searching for work and food. War in Europe was not far away.

Fireside Chats

To combat the mood of despair, Roosevelt turned to a powerful new weapon: radio. The very first week of his presidency he gave his first "fireside chat," and a series of such chats helped him pull the nation through its hard times.

Warm and personal in tone, the book of Deuteronomy resembles just such a fireside chat, delivered by the great leader Moses to his people, the Israelites. He, too, led a nation through dangerous times, and at the end of his life he had many parting words. This book is Moses' State of the Union address, personal diary, and tearful swansong all combined into one.

Poised on the Edge

For their length and emotional power, these speeches have no equal in the Bible. Moses passionately went over and over the same ground, occasionally lashing out, but more often showing the anguish and love of a doting parent. An undercurrent of sadness runs through the speeches: Moses knew he would not join in the triumph of entering Canaan. God had revealed that Moses would die before then.

In Exodus, Moses was marked by a quick temper and a reluctance to speak. His humility and eloquence as seen in Deuteronomy show how far he had come in 40 years.

Deep in his soul, Moses felt that the entire history of the Jews depended on what happened next. Poised on the banks of the Jordan River, they were about to enter the promised land and face the most crucial test of their lives. How would they react to the new land? Would they keep their covenant with God or reject it for the more immediate pleasures around them?

Desert-bred, the Israelites knew little about the seductions of other cultures: the sensuality, the exotic religions, the glittering wealth. They had spent their lives in near-isolation, sheltered from civilization. Now they were marching into a land full of enticements.

Three Speeches

Moses' first great speech, in chapters 1-3, reviewed God's dealings with Israel. Moses recalled Israel's history through his own eyes, mentioning such details as the irrigation system in Egypt, the abrupt departure, the fearsome desert with its serpents and scorpions, and the amazing miracles of God. He filled the account with personal reflections, like an aging father telling his children what to remember after he is gone.

The longest speech, chapters 4-26, went over the moral and civil code the Israelites had agreed to keep. Even here, a personal tone came through. Moses did not list laws as in a textbook; he discussed and amplified and preached them. Along with the laws, he included reminders, object lessons, personal outbursts.

In chapters 27-33 Moses gave a final summing up, a farewell charge from an old man facing certain death. As clearly as he could, he presented the choices facing the Israelites. He would not be with them as they chose their future. They were on their own; they held their destiny in their own hands.

How to Read Deuteronomy

Early in this century archaeologists began turning up samples of Near Eastern treaties. These "suzerainty treaties" set down in official form the relationship between a powerful king and the people he ruled over. Such treaties shed new light on the book of Deuteronomy, which seems to follow very closely the pattern of such a treaty. Typically, a treaty with a powerful king consisted of the following elements:

1. *A preamble identifying the parties of the treaty,* such as a king and a small cluster of tribes who want his protection.

2. *A capsule history describing previous relations between the two parties.*

3. *Rules defining each party's obligations.* The king may swear to defend some tribes with his armies in return for allegiance, taxes, and a percentage of produce.

4. *Witnesses to the treaties,* including, in many cases, a list of gods.

5. *Curses and blessings specifying what will take place if one of the parties breaks the treaty.* The king may promise the people prosperity and peace if they keep the terms, but invasion, deportation, or death if they break them.

Read Deuteronomy as an example of a treaty between a king and his people. *Treaty* is another word for the one we have been using—*covenant*—to describe the formal agreement between God and the Israelites. With a little work, you can identify various portions of Deuteronomy that parallel the five elements above.

Chapters 1-11 and 27-34 contain the best summary of Moses' speeches to the Israelites. He holds back no emotion as he retells the story of his life. Almost all the action he describes repeats what we've heard before (see Exodus 12-20; 32-34; Numbers 11-17; 20-24), but Deuteronomy provides a much more personal account.

Unlike other ancient books, the Bible gives major emphasis to "nobodies"—poor people, aliens, widows, orphans, the sick. Many of the laws relating to them repeat laws from the three preceding books. But Deuteronomy gives hidden insights into why God has such special concern for nobodies and why the Israelites should also. It also gives intriguing ideas on how such concern can be translated into actual political and economic policies. As you go through the book, mark each passage that relates to such people.

The New Testament quotes Deuteronomy more often than any other Old Testament book. Twenty-one of the 27 New Testament books allude to Deuteronomy; some scholars count 90 different citations. Jesus, himself, drew from it during his temptation (Matthew 4).

Notes

_____

_____

_____

_____

_____

JOSHUA

INTRODUCTION

The Difference 40 Years Can Make

They faced overwhelming odds with renewed hope

On the surface, not much had changed in 40 years. The band of refugees amassing beside the Jordan River greatly resembled a similar horde from four decades before. They had panicked once. Would they again?

The Israelites still faced overwhelming odds. They had no chariots or even horses. They had only primitive arms, an untested new leader, and long-delayed marching orders from God.

A New Spirit, a New Leader

Yet, in another sense, everything had changed. Older Israelites with fearful, slave mentalities had died off in the desert—all the older generation except Joshua and Caleb, two legendary warriors. The new generation had decided to trust God, no matter what. In stark contrast to the spies in Numbers (13:31-33), Joshua's scouts brought back this report, "The Lord has surely given the whole land into our hands; all the people are melting in fear because of us" (2:24).

The book of Joshua contains not a word about rebellion against a leader or grumbling against God. It is a good news book, a welcome relief from the discouraging tone of Numbers and the fatalism of Deuteronomy. What a difference 40 years had made!

As newly appointed leader of the Israelites, Joshua took on two main tasks. First, he was to direct a military campaign to take control of the land God had promised. Then, he would parcel out the conquered land among all the tribes.

Learning to Follow Instructions

Once inside Canaan, the Israelites followed God's instructions precisely, even when doing so must have strained their faith to new limits. The residents of Jericho had shut themselves behind stone walls, awaiting the onslaught of the feared Israelites. But how did the Israelites spend their first week in Canaan? They built a stone monument to God, performed circumcision rituals, and held a Passover celebration. No conquering army had ever behaved in such a manner.

Everything in Joshua seems handpicked to strike home the point that God was really in charge. Covering a period of approximately seven years, Joshua's 24 chapters devote only a few sentences to some extensive military campaigns (see chapters 10-11). But key events, such as the fall of Jericho, get detailed coverage, underscoring that the Israelites succeeded when they relied on God, not military might. The few negative stories (such as the battle of Ai and the trick of the Gibeonites) show what happened when the Israelites did not seek God's will.

A Book of Hope

The Bible does not give history for its own sake. Rather, it presents practical and spiritual lessons. Fortunately, Joshua's lessons are overwhelmingly positive ones. Guided by God, the nation of Israel met with unprecedented success. In fact, the book concludes that "not one of all the Lord's good promises to the house of Israel failed; every one was fulfilled" (21:45).

The book of Joshua gives a fresh breeze of hope. Writers of hymns and spirituals have often gone back to it to try to recapture the spirit of success that swept over God's people those first few years in the new land. It *can* work: people can follow God. Joshua shows how.

How to Read Joshua

Phrases in the first two paragraphs of Joshua hint at the tone to follow. "I will never leave you nor forsake you," God promised. "I will give you every place where you set foot." "Be careful to obey all the law my servant Moses gave you . . . that you may be successful wherever you go."

Often the Israelites offer examples of what *not* to do. Already the books of Exodus, Numbers, and Deuteronomy have given negative examples, and the historical books to follow will describe further failures in lurid detail. But the Old Testament does offer a few bright spots of hope, the book of Joshua being one of the brightest.

(The "good news" character of Joshua causes some people to compare it to the New Testament books of Ephesians and Philippians, which share its success-and-triumph tone. You may want to read one of those New Testament books along with Joshua.)

Fast-paced battle action appears in chapters 1-11, "the book of war." The latter chapters, "the book of distribution," mostly concern the parceling out of the land.

You can casually read about the military campaigns of Joshua, but to truly appreciate them you must study a map or Bible atlas. Joshua is a very geographical book. Place-names appear in every chapter, describing the military progress and also the division of the land among the tribes of Israel.

As you read Joshua, keep two major themes in mind: Joshua's leadership and God's direct involvement in history. Study Joshua's life as an example of leadership. What were the reasons behind his few failures, such as those recorded in chapters 7 and 9? You may also want to refer to the background passages on his life in Exodus (17, 24, 32, 33) and Numbers (11, 13, 26). What lesson did Joshua learn at each of these key moments?

Notes

_____

_____

_____

_____

_____

JUDGES

INTRODUCTION

Freedom Fighters

These "judges" took up arms to defend their homeland

The "judges" of this book might be called guerrillas or freedom fighters today. These men (and one woman) were renowned not for court cases, but for their military campaigns against foreign invaders. Like all military leaders, they sometimes settled disputes; the book of Judges, however, is preoccupied not with legal matters, but with the excitement of fighting for freedom.

Israel's judges certainly did not stick to "the rules of proper warfare." Judge Ehud tricked his opponent into a private conference; behind closed doors he pulled out a knife and plunged it into the enemy king's belly (3:12-30). Judge Gideon won a surprise victory in the middle of the night. His small band so confused the occupying army with noise and lights that the enemy soldiers stabbed each other and fled in the darkness (chapter 7). Samson never led an army; his battle tricks have been compared to the pranks of an overgrown juvenile delinquent (chapters 14-16).

Most of the time the Israelites hid in the hills while their enemies, with superior weapons, controlled the plains. (Chariots, like tanks, were devastating in level country, but almost useless in muddy or rugged terrain.) Outnumbered, the Israelites relied on ambushes and sneak attacks. They knew every gully, for they were fighting for their homeland. Strategy made up for lack of strength.

Ugliest Stories of the Bible

As a book about early Jewish military heroes, Judges inspires and fascinates. But you can't make the whole book fit that description. If you read strictly looking for heroes, you'd have to ignore half of Judges—and you would miss its most important point about God's work with Israel.

For one thing, Judges' "heroes" were badly flawed. Samson was pitifully vulnerable to his lust for women. Gideon won a battle, then led the nation into idolatry. Jephthah, a former outlaw, apparently knew very little about the God he was supposed to serve.

Add to this the "non-heroic" material: Abimelech, Gideon's son, who slaughtered 70 half-brothers so he could be named king; Jephthah and Gideon, who massacred fellow Israelites who had failed to support them; and the sad characters of the last five chapters of Judges. These contain some of the ugliest stories in the Bible—tales of homosexual assault, idolatry, civil war, thievery, rape, and murder. The book of Judges runs downhill, from bad to worse. You may end up wondering what such material is doing in the Bible.

Every picture has shadows; every suspenseful novel has chapters that look truly dark. In the story of God and his people, Judges is that kind of chapter. Heroes appear sporadically, but humanity remains terribly unheroic.

Enthusiasm Fades

God wanted better things for his people than he got in Judges. He had rescued Israel from slavery in Egypt. He had given them a rich land and presented them with a grand system of worship and government centering on him. He would be no distant God in the heavens—he would live with them.

But after some initial enthusiasm, the Israelites didn't continue the way God had pointed. Instead, they learned to live with the sophisticated people they found as their neighbors—people whose faults included worshiping idols through sex orgies and child sacrifice.

The Israelites held the mountains, but the foreign-held valleys, cutting through the land, separated the tribes. Soon each group of isolated Israelites began operating independently. The next generation lost its sense of national identity. The people worshiped the idol Baal alongside the Lord. Though descended from 12 brothers, they spent more time fighting each other than the foreign oppressors. They violated virtually every moral standard. The last verse of Judges sums it up: "Everyone did as he saw fit." What they saw fit, wasn't.

The Secret of Their Survival

The foreign invasions were no accident, Judges says: they came from God just as surely as the heroic rescuers did. A pattern developed. God allowed suffering as a consequence of the Israelites' disobedience. When things grew really terrible, their attention would turn back to God. He would respond by sending a judge to rescue them. But soon they would fail again. This pattern repeated itself time and again. The Israelites always forgot their need for God, and the dreary cycle ground on.

The secret of Israel's survival was not, then, military heroes or guerrilla tactics. It was the persistent, unwearied love of God himself. Though they forgot him, he did not forget them. He gave innumerable new beginnings. Again and again he sent "judges" to rescue them. He would not let them go. God is the real hero of Judges.

How to Read Judges

You can read Judges as a collection of heroic stories, the most famous of which are Gideon's and Samson's. But together the tales tell a less heroic story.

Read Judges, therefore, on two levels at once. On one level focus on the new beginning God repeatedly offered by sending a judge to rescue Israel. These are character stories with great fascination. You can gain a great deal by studying the strengths and weaknesses of the individual judges.

On another level, read of the deterioration of a nation that quickly forgot what God had done for it. This will help you understand why, in the next stage of Israel's history, God gave the Israelites a king.

Notes

_____

_____

_____

_____

_____

A Rare Bond of Love

Ruth and Naomi lost everything, except their care for each other

Ruth and Naomi were unlikely friends: a generation apart, one young and strong, the other past middle age. Stranger still, one was the other's mother-in-law and came from a completely different ethnic and religious background. Who would have put them together?

They had lost everything when their husbands died. With no man to rely on, their lives were at risk in those rough times. No one else would come to their defense: they had only each other.

The Woman's Initiative

The book of Ruth is not "two women against the world." Rather, it shows the women taking initiative to find, by God's help, a man who would care for them.

A woman's initiative rarely gets so direct as in Ruth. At her mother-in-law's direction Ruth located where Boaz, a relative, was camping out. She waited until dark, then crept to his feet and lay down. When Boaz woke and found her, he didn't have to be told what was on her mind. She wanted him for a husband. Flattered, he didn't let another sun set before making the legal arrangements for marriage.

Society the way God had designed it encouraged men like Boaz to help the needy. For instance, by Old Testament law a farmer had to leave some of his grain behind so that poor people like Ruth could harvest it. And, also by law, a helpless widow had to be taken into the home of her husband's family. This was the law by which Boaz claimed Ruth (4:1-12).

God's Invisible Presence

Behind the eloquent story of Ruth looms an invisible helper—God. He didn't intervene in the events, so far as the story tells. But nobody in Ruth doubted that life proceeded under God's direction. It was the Lord by whom Ruth swore when declaring her love to Naomi (1:17), and the Lord whom Naomi credited for bringing Ruth to Boaz's field (2:20). God's law brought Boaz and Ruth into marriage. Finally, the Lord gave them a son, in whom mother, father, and "grandmother" found deep satisfaction.

The last verses of Ruth show, furthermore, that God's plan extended beyond Ruth and Naomi's personal problems. Ruth was a member of the despised Moabites—enemies of Israel. Yet God not only accepted her into his family, but also used her to produce Israel's greatest king. Ruth's great-grandson turned out to be David. To anyone who thought that God's love was for Jews only, Ruth's life made a striking contradiction.

How to Read Ruth

Ruth, brief enough to read in 15 minutes, is a delight. The German poet Goethe called it "the loveliest complete work on a small scale." But because Ruth's author didn't hammer his points home, it is possible to overlook his deeper meaning. As you read, concentrate on the loving bond between Ruth and Naomi. This love, which thrived in suffering, is the root of the book. It offers hope for other people in hard circumstances.

The author of Ruth assumed that readers understood the cultural and historical background of Ruth's time. You may wish to read about it for deeper understanding. Deuteronomy 25:5-10 describes the background on marriage for a widow by a member of her husband's family, the "kinsman-redeemer." Leviticus 25:23-28 gives background on a poor person's property. The Introduction to Judges offers historical perspective, for the book of Judges is an overview of the brutal times Ruth lived in.

Notes

_____

_____

_____

_____

_____

1 SAMUEL

INTRODUCTION

What Leadership Requires

Israel, fighting for survival, needed a leader

No country, no organization, no family is great without great leadership. But how do you get it? Israel was forced to ask that question during a critical, do-or-die period. Three men rose to the highest power: Samuel, Saul, and David. All were attractive, powerful figures who commanded admiration and respect. Two, David and Samuel, made very successful leaders. The other, Saul, had a promising beginning but ended as a failure.

Fighting for Survival

Israel was fighting for survival. The Philistines had migrated to the region about the same time Israel had escaped from Egypt. Now, from their cities near the Mediterranean coast, they were gradually pushing deeper into the mountains of Israel. They had superior weapons—chariots, in particular. Though less populous than Israel, they were apparently better organized.

Israel had neither central administration nor a regular army. A loose confederation of 12 tribes, Israelites called on each other for help only in emergencies. Occasional inspired leaders—"judges"—took charge of military defense when necessary. The nation had worked that way for well over 100 years, and the tribes seemed too independent to change. But the Philistines were pressing them. A crisis of leadership—a crisis testing the very existence of Israel—was building.

Why Begin with Hannah?

Surprisingly, 1 Samuel opens not with a battle or even with the leadership crisis, but with a very private family problem. Two bitterly jealous wives had a longstanding quarrel, one taunting the other because of her infertility. Hannah, the childless woman, turned to God in desperation, praying and promising to dedicate a son to him. The result was a little boy named Samuel.

Hannah kept her vow to God, and Samuel grew into one of the greatest leaders Israel had ever known. He had a triple role: he served as a prophet who could discern God's will, as a priest who led Israel to worship, and as a military leader. He chose, under God's direction, Israel's first two kings. Samuel's strong personality undergirds the entire book of 1 Samuel, even though he officially retired at the end of chapter 15.

Why begin 1 Samuel with Hannah? Hannah's struggles are Israel's, in miniature. Her frustration forced her to look to God, and as a result her son Samuel served in the tabernacle instead of following in his father's footsteps as a farmer. Hannah's story shows that from bitter pain may come great promise, if that pain leads you to God. The Israelites, who were going to experience a great many more troubles in their history, needed Hannah's example.

God Chooses His Own Leaders

Hannah's story also reminds us that God's leaders don't necessarily come through regulation channels. Ordinarily, Eli's corrupt sons would have carried on national leadership. But God wanted no part of them. Instead, he blessed a woman who had turned to him in her troubles, and he blessed her son as long as that son trusted in him for help. God chose a leader to suit himself, a leader who listened to him. "The LORD declares: 'Those who honor me I will honor, but those who despise me will be disdained'" (2:30).

Samuel never forgot that lesson. He anointed Saul as the first king, and then, when Saul failed to honor God, stripped him of his authority. Passing over many impressive men, Samuel chose David, a young shepherd, to replace Saul. Under David, Israel would be transformed into a wealthy, secure kingdom. Was this because David had such natural leadership qualities? First Samuel suggests a different perspective: David succeeded because God chose him for the job, and because David persistently turned to God for his direction. The best leadership, ultimately, belongs to God.

How to Read 1 Samuel

Some of the stories of 1 Samuel—David and Goliath, for instance—are justly famous as great adventures. But you should read for more than excitement. Look for insights into the character required for leadership. Samuel and David were great leaders. Saul, on the other hand, was a miserable failure.

These men led Israel during a crucial, bloody period. Israel had been dominated by a foreign power and, partly because of this, was changing its government to a monarchy. This change in governmental institutions, along with tribal tensions, form the background for the book. A good commentary can help explain this, but you can get much of it for yourself by asking, as you read, three questions: What are the most important national problems facing Israel? What kind of leadership is needed? How do these three leaders (and numerous smaller figures) respond to these needs?

Notes

_____

_____

_____

_____

_____

2 SAMUEL

INTRODUCTION

The Life of King David

From herding sheep to ruling a nation

The Bible is filled with strong personalities, but none leads David in the parade. His life was a whirlwind, from which striking images flash. We see him playing his harp, writing poems, fighting battles, faking insanity, dancing jubilantly in praise of God. We watch his tear-streaked face when he learns of his closest friend's death. We see him on his rooftop, gazing down lustfully on Bathsheba's bath. We see Nathan point his finger at him, accusing him of adultery and murder. We hear David's guilty, anguished voice crying to God for the life of his infant child. We see David's bowed head as he stumbles out of Jerusalem, pursued by his murderous son.

David survived the crises of a dozen lives. Somehow he always bounced back. Somehow he maintained a passionate trust in God. First and Second Samuel don't paint him as a flawless character, nor as a perfect model of strength and courage. David had striking weaknesses. Yet he appeals to us as he did to the Israelites: he was completely, passionately alive. Whatever he did, right or wrong, he did with his whole heart. In his love for God, he held nothing back.

Healing the Wounds of War

While 1 Samuel tells of David's youth and his long exile, 2 Samuel focuses on David as king, leading, uniting, inspiring his people. His time in the desert was over. Different qualities of leadership were required in a king.

David inherited a country in tatters. His fellow Southerners recognized him as the new king. But Saul's son, backed by a powerful general, launched a civil war for the throne. Ugly infighting followed: intrigue, murder, and treachery.

Even after David's rivals were eliminated, peace was uneasy. Unless David could heal the wounds of war, resentment might smolder in the hearts of the Northerners. David's decisive action showed wisdom and firmness. He justly punished murderers who expected his gratitude. He showed respect for his enemies by mourning their deaths. From his first day in office David behaved as the king of all the people, not just his loyal followers. The Northern tribes soon came over to him, submitting to his leadership (5:1-3).

David's next move was to capture Jerusalem. People said it couldn't be done; mountainous Jerusalem was impregnable. David did it, and made Jerusalem his new political and religious capital. Located on the border between North and South, Jerusalem symbolized a new national unity based on trust in God.

That was just the beginning. David led the unified tribes to do what they had barely dreamed of: they defeated the dreaded Philistines once and for all. Almost overnight the tiny, threatened nation of Israel became safe. Secure borders opened expanded trade, and Israel boomed. (David's son Solomon reaped most of the wealth from this.) Naturally, David's popularity increased.

A Murderer and an Adulterer

But David's reign held ironic tragedies, too. Second Samuel makes no effort to hide them. David could lead a nation but not his own children. His ineffective parenting nearly destroyed all he had done when his heartless son Absalom led a rebellion. Second Samuel portrays David without retouching his blemishes: he was a murderer and an adulterer and a leader capable of cruelty.

Nevertheless, he was Israel's greatest king. Even at his lowest points, his great strength of character showed. He was never vengeful with his enemies. He took full responsibility for his mistakes. He managed to remember that he had started out as a mere shepherd. He held power only by the grace of God—and he believed that God had every right to take power away.

Through his love for God and his sense of astonished gratefulness for what God had done for him, David became a living embodiment of the Israel God wanted. Like all truly great leaders, he made his country thrive not just by what he did, but by who he was.

How to Read 2 Samuel

Second Samuel continues, without a break, the story begun in 1 Samuel—the two were originally one book. The difference is that David, who once sought only to survive, now seeks to unify a badly divided country. His greater responsibilities put extra stress on his leadership qualities. You can study his life with leadership in mind. You can also study chapters 11-20 to see the cancerous effects of a leader's private sins and poor family leadership.

Chapters 21-24 seem to be an appendix, bringing in other important events and facts of David's reign. Much of 2 Samuel's story is also told in 1 Chronicles 11-21, often word for word the same.

Notes

_____

_____

_____

_____

_____

1 KINGS

INTRODUCTION

The Man Who Had Everything

The richest, wisest, most successful person of his time

The first half of 1 Kings describes a man who got life handed to him on a silver platter. The son of King David and Queen Bathsheba, young Solomon grew up in the royal palace. Early on, he astounded others with his talent for songwriting and natural history. He composed 1,005 songs and spun off 3,000 proverbs (a sampling of which were collected in the biblical book of Proverbs).

Solomon became king of Israel and received from God the special gift of wisdom. He was called the wisest man in the world, and kings and queens traveled hundreds of miles to meet him. They went away dazzled by the genius of Israel's king and by the prosperity of his nation.

The Best Years Ever

Israel reached its Golden Age under King Solomon, a time forever remembered with nostalgia by Jews. Almost all the promised land lay in Israel's hands, and the nation was at peace. Literature and culture flourished. Of the people, the Bible records simply that "they ate, they drank and they were happy" (4:20). "The king made silver as common in Jerusalem as stones" (10:27).

Of all Solomon's accomplishments, one stands out above the others. He built the temple of God, the finest building in the world of that day. Almost 200,000 men labored for seven years to complete it.

Despite the successes of Solomon's reign, however, later in his life the king had a dramatic downturn. His fall eventually brought the kingdom crashing down around him, and the second half of 1 Kings describes the grim process of dismemberment.

What Went Wrong?

How did it happen? How could the liveliest, wealthiest, most contented nation of its day slide so disastrously in one generation?

As 1 Kings tells it, Solomon seemed unable to control his excesses. Reared in a palace, he loved luxury. When Israel launched its first maritime expeditions, he used them to gather such exotica as gold, ivory, apes, peacocks, and silver. He plated the floor of the temple with gold, wastefully gilded over fine cedar and precious ivory, and fashioned militarily useless shields out of gold. First Kings describes the seven-year construction of the temple in elaborate detail. But then it pointedly notes that the construction of Solomon's palace—twice the temple's size—took 13 years (7:1).

Solomon showed similar extravagance in his love life. First, he married the daughter of the Egyptian pharaoh (perhaps indicating he was relying on military alliances, not God, for the defense of his country). Then, disobeying God's specific orders, he married the princesses of Moab, Ammon, Edom, Sidon, and other nations. Seven hundred wives in all, and 300 concubines! The entire complexion of the court changed. It became un-Jewish, foreign. To please his wives, Solomon took a final, terrible step: he built altars to all their gods. The one who had built the Israelites' greatest monument to God had fallen to worshiping idols.

Rumblings of Discontent in the Land

To pay for the building projects, Solomon instituted Israel's first national taxation system. He drafted workers for employment and kept them as virtual slaves. When bills mounted, he went so far as to cede certain northern towns in the promised land to another king (9:10-14). Resentment opened up between Israel's North and South.

But the gulf separating Israel from God was even more dangerous. Previously, the people of Israel had looked to God as their leader. Now, however, the focus shifted from God in heaven to the king in Jerusalem. Solomon had even made himself the unofficial religious leader of the country, and when he slid badly, the nation soon followed.

Solomon started out with every advantage of wealth, power, and wisdom. But 1 Kings gives this tragic conclusion: "So Solomon did evil in the eyes of the LORD; he did not follow the LORD completely, as David his father had done" (11:6).

Solomon seemed obsessed with a desire to outdo anyone who had ever lived. Along the way, he failed to make God the center of his life. He achieved lasting fame in history, but as a negative example. Jesus Christ himself rendered the final verdict on Solomon and his striving for glory when he pointed to a lily growing wild in the field. "Not even Solomon in all his splendor," he said, "was dressed like one of these" (Matthew 6:29).

How to Read 1 Kings

First and Second Kings were originally one book: the same Hebrew scroll contained both. Hebrew, having no vowels, is a very compact language, and when the book of Kings was translated into the wordier Greek and Latin, more space was needed. Translators arbitrarily split Kings. The two books, however, should be read as one.

First divides neatly almost in half, with mostly good news in the first half. It tells of Israel's Golden Age, when King Solomon brought peace and prosperity to the nation. But he also sowed the seed for the calamities to follow. Chapter 12 marks the beginning of a civil war that ruptured Israel into two nations: Israel in the North and Judah in the South. The rest of Kings describes, ruler by ruler, the reigns of 19 kings in the North and 19 kings and one queen in the South.

Another book, 2 Chronicles, covers the exact same historical period as the book of Kings. In some cases, 2 Chronicles adds more detail, so if a story interests you, read the parallel account there. These books of history form the background for 17 other books of the Bible: the Prophets. Famous prophets such as Isaiah, Jeremiah, Hosea, and Amos preached during the time of Kings.

Keeping 39 rulers straight can seem hopeless, especially since the book jumps back and forth between two countries. Remember:

> Israel was the Northern Kingdom, with its capital in Samaria. Its kings were all unfaithful to God.
> Judah was the Southern Kingdom, with its capital in Jerusalem. Almost half of its rulers remained somewhat faithful to God; the others proved disobedient.

Notes

_____

_____

_____

_____

_____

2 KINGS

INTRODUCTION

The Great Wars of Israel

The promised land turns into a bloody battlefield

The book of 2 Kings tells of dark days in the promised land. First, the Northern Kingdom, Israel, fell to outside invaders. Then Judah, the Southern Kingdom, was conquered. To appreciate what those two events meant in Jewish history, consider our century's two great wars.

In 1918 the bloodiest war of all time came to an end. The entire planet had chosen sides. In all, nine million soldiers died. Survivors thought nothing could ever again match The Great War's ferocity and destruction. "The war to end all wars," they called it.

Yet, in a mere 20 years, a man named Adolf Hitler brought war again. In World War II, global violence stretched from London in the West to Japan in the East. The war finally closed with a blinding mushroom cloud, an ominous portent for the future.

Two Large Blots in History

No matter what else happens, the 20th century has been permanently stained by those two large blots: World War I and World War II. Everything else—art, literature, advances in science and medicine—fades into the background.

As 2 Kings tells it, something very similar occurred in the biblical nation of Israel. Two large blots spread across the land: successive invasions by foreign giants. In the long, turbulent history of the Jews, these two invasions stand out as the Great Wars, overshadowing nearly everything else.

Israel Falls First

The kingdom had already split into two—1 Kings tells that story. Its sequel, 2 Kings, describes ever-increasing tragedy.

From the very first chapters you can sense the pending crisis in the North. Not one Northern king followed the ways of God. National politics slipped into an endless cycle of intrigue and bloody revolt. Meanwhile, Elijah and Elisha intensified their attacks on the kings, and miracles broke out with unusual frequency.

Assyria's campaigns—the "World War I" in Israel's history—are reported in 2 Kings 15-18. Other records of the period tell of vicious fighting. Samaria, Israel's capital, made one final heroic stand against a two-year siege. Finally, the starving survivors surrendered, and the people of Israel were carried away into captivity.

Only two Israelite tribes remained in the promised land, holding out in the tiny Southern Kingdom of Judah. Ultimately, King Sennacherib of Assyria turned against Judah also, penetrating all the way to the gates of Jerusalem. He leveled 46 walled cities and carried away 200,150 people, young and old, along with all their horses, mules, cattle, and possessions. He scornfully dismissed King Hezekiah as "a bird in a cage."

A Brief Comeback

Could the tiny nation of Judah survive such an onslaught? Somehow the "caged bird" (Hezekiah) made a remarkable comeback, and Judah did survive for another 135 years. Still, Judah did not learn from the dramatic object lesson of Israel's destruction in the North. Most of the kings who followed Hezekiah failed dismally to obey God. Another foreign invader, Babylon, finally leveled Jerusalem in the "World War II" of that era.

The book of Kings ends with a bleak picture: refugees picking through the rubble of Jerusalem, and the Israelites enslaved by foreign powers. The temple itself, God's house, lay in ruins, its treasures carted off to Babylon. When the dust settled around 600 B.C., the Israelites were scattered across the earth, not to be reunited as an independent nation for 25 centuries.

All along, prophets had given eloquent warnings of what would happen to a nation that turned its back on God. But nothing makes a bigger impact than the object lesson of history itself. Ever since, Jews have looked back upon their history and seen two indelible stains. Those were the dark days of Assyria and Babylon, when everything came apart.

How to Read 2 Kings

The first eight chapters of 2 Kings, full of excitement and adventure, read easily. They focus on the last days of the prophet Elijah and on the long life of his successor Elisha. But beginning with chapter 9, the book can become very confusing. It switches back and forth between two histories: that of Israel in the North and Judah in the South.

Israel was strong initially, with 10 of the 12 tribes united there. But it proved less faithful to God and was ultimately destroyed by Assyria. Chapters 18-25 cover the period after the Assyrian invasion, when only Judah existed.

One important reason for studying the books of Kings and Chronicles is that they give historical background on the prophets. Elijah and Elisha appeared at a crucial turning point in the history of the Northern Kingdom, just as Ahab was changing the official religion from worship of God to worship of Baal. Other prophets, who wrote books of the Bible, were also active during this time.

Amos and Hosea concentrated their work in the Northern Kingdom of Israel. The following prophets lived and preached in the Southern Kingdom of Judah: Obadiah, Joel, Isaiah, Micah, Nahum, Zephaniah, Jeremiah, and Habakkuk. More prophets came later, when the Israelites were still captive in Babylon or after they returned to their homeland.

Second Kings, like its companion books, makes brief and sweeping judgments of each king or queen. As you read, look for what pleased God and what displeased him. The 39 rulers comprise a fine study of leadership of all kinds, from the inspiring to the degenerate.

Notes

_____

_____

_____

_____

_____

1 CHRONICLES

INTRODUCTION

A Family Record

These facts reminded Israelites of their place in God's plan

In pioneer days, many American families prized a huge black family Bible. Often the only book in the house, it served for more than reading. It was also the family memory bank. Every important event—a marriage, a birth, a death—was recorded on its flyleaves. The Bible was passed down from generation to generation, and through it, a family kept track of its past.

The book of 1 Chronicles is something like that—a record of Israel's family history, and particularly of David, Israel's greatest king. In fact, at first glance, 1 Chronicles looks like a rehash of David's life as told in 2 Samuel and 1 Kings. Some of the most dramatic episodes in David's life—his clash with Goliath, his sin with Bathsheba—don't make it into this account. But David's organization of the temple is told in great detail, and long lists and genealogies fill over half the book.

Because of that, few people read 1 Chronicles. Most of us are more interested in personalities than in institutions and genealogies.

David's Lasting Impact

First Chronicles, however, is far more interested in David's lasting accomplishments than in his ups and downs as an individual. The nation he led was more than a collection of inspired individuals. It was founded on God's unshakable promises to the children of Abraham. He had promised to be with them. He had promised to provide leadership. He had promised to make them a blessing to the world. These promises took shape in enduring institutions—the temple and the monarchy, most notably.

Why a List of Names?

The first nine chapters of 1 Chronicles trace the genealogy of Israel back to Adam. The author brings together more family records than you'll find anywhere else in the Bible. These records helped the Israelites remember their position as members in God's chosen family. God had given them unique ways to follow and worship him. First Chronicles reminded the Israelites—as it reminds us—of how different their family was meant to be.

How to Read 1 Chronicles

Few will enjoy reading 1 Chronicles's many lists and genealogies straight through. You should approach them more like a puzzle. Don't get lost in the hundreds of names. Instead, try to understand how the different parts of 1 Chronicles fit together. For each section ask, "Why was this included? What did it mean to the original audience—to the Israelites who had returned from exile in Babylon? How did it encourage them as they made a new beginning?"

First Chronicles divides cleanly into two parts. The first nine chapters are mainly lists of names. In these, the Israelites read their family tree and discovered their heritage. Chapters 10 to 29 tell David's story, focusing on the legacy he left behind for future generations—especially the temple. David, a founding father of Israel, transformed the nation in a way that lasted hundreds of years.

Notes

_____
_____
_____
_____
_____

2 CHRONICLES

INTRODUCTION

A Time for Hope

Restoring pride to a group of refugees

In the early 1960s, a wave of feeling known as "black pride" swept across America. It started when black leaders realized that far more than legal rights had been repressed for 200 years. Everything about the black culture, from hair texture to history, had taken a back seat to that of the white majority.

Over time, a dramatic rediscovery of the black heritage occurred. Textbook publishers issued new editions that for the first time included the stories of black Americans: a soldier who rowed George Washington across the Delaware, a scientist who perfected the process of blood transfusion, an educator who founded black colleges.

Black pride reminded all Americans that a minority race had made giant contributions in many fields. Black people encountered a heritage they had known little about. Heroes were uncovered. Blacks everywhere began to see the past in a new light.

Need for a Pep Talk

There was a time when the Israelites, too, desperately needed a new look at the past. Their ancestors had also been torn from home, beaten, and dragged off in chains to serve as slaves in a foreign country. In Babylon, a new generation grew up knowing little of the Israelite past: the covenant with God, the promised line of kings, the magnificent temple in Jerusalem.

When captive Israelites were finally allowed to return home, they found a pile of rubble. In Israel's Golden Age, people had traveled thousands of miles to view the majesty of Jerusalem and its temple. But to the refugees' horror, not one stone of the temple remained standing. The carved beams had all been hacked to pieces, the gold and ivory stripped away, and the furniture auctioned off or destroyed.

Outside the capital, whole villages had disappeared. Vital religious customs had gone uncelebrated for 70 years. Jewish culture was in danger of leaking away.

The book of Chronicles was written to those refugees who returned. For that dispirited group of people, the author recounted the glory days of Israel. He wanted to restore pride in the Israelite past, and bring hope to their future.

History in a New Light

Chronicles (both 1 and 2) thus retells history, starting all the way at the beginning, with Adam. Most of the characters are familiar, but Chronicles tells old stories in a new light. Its author isn't just reciting facts. He is delivering a word of bright hope, a pep talk, to just-freed refugees.

Some accuse Chronicles of being a "whitewashed" history, especially in comparison to the Bible's other history books. True, the book barely mentions the Israelites' great failures—it says nothing of David's or Solomon's mistakes, for instance. Presumably, the refugees had heard plenty about the dark side of their nation's recent past: the books of Samuel and Kings, which ruthlessly exposed those failures, had been around for years.

Similarly, Chronicles ignores the chaotic Northern Kingdom of Israel, and the civil war Judah waged against it. Nothing remained of the ten scattered tribes of the North, and the book wastes little space on them. Instead, Chronicles reaches higher, seeking to restore pride in the original ideals of the nation.

A Distant Hope

The good kings of Judah, eight in all, dominate the story: over two-thirds of 2 Chronicles is devoted to their reigns. Chronicles focuses on God's special relationship with the Israelites, recalling the covenant that had brought about their Golden Age. It reviews the religious reforms led by each king, and, above all, highlights the temple, the house where God's presence came to rest. If God had lived among them in the past, couldn't he do so again?

How to Read 2 Chronicles

You will recognize many of the stories in 2 Chronicles—about half of it closely follows other Bible passages. The author freely admits he has relied on the books of Moses, Samuel, and Kings. He also quotes from Judges, Jeremiah, the Psalms, Isaiah, and Lamentations, as well as many books that have been lost to history.

But 2 Chronicles does not merely repeat. It weaves together stories and facts for a specific purpose: a Jewish philosophy of history. Chronicles sheds new light on that history by highlighting rare moments of peace and prosperity. Worship of the true God had made Israel strong. As you read, notice how 2 Chronicles underscores that fact by stressing the temple and the priests.

Notes

_____

_____

_____

_____

_____

INTRODUCTION

Beginning Again

For the exiles from Babylon, news almost too good to be true

Ezra begins with exiles returning to a ruined city—a brush-covered ghost town burned and pillaged nearly 50 years before by an overpowering Babylonian army. Would Jerusalem now have a new beginning?

Psalm 126 captures the returning exiles' feelings: "We were like men who dreamed. Our mouths were filled with laughter, our tongues with songs of joy." The Persian Empire had conquered mighty Babylon and, under the emperor Cyrus, offered all Jews a chance to return to their land. It was too good to believe.

A New Start with God

One poet in exile had written, "If I forget you, O Jerusalem, may my right hand forget its skill" (Psalm 137:5). These returned exiles were the minority who, decades afterwards, had not forgotten. They treasured their spiritual heritage more than the houses and businesses they had built in Babylon. They wanted to live and worship in the place God had given his people. Any sacrifice was worth this opportunity. Their first impulse when they arrived was to rebuild the temple, God's home.

The tolerant Persians (whose official policy was to encourage the local religion in every area they governed) had even brought out the silver and gold temple articles, carefully preserved in a Babylonian temple as though waiting on God's timing. When the returned exiles laid the foundation to the new temple, the sound of their shouting (and noisy weeping) could be heard from far away (3:13). The temple, after all, was the place where they would meet God. It symbolized a new start with him.

The Problems of Beginning Again

God had opened the way, but the exiles needed determination to follow it. The book of Ezra divides into three parts, each one dealing with an obstacle that arose. The first part tells how, immediately after the return of the exiles, their neighbors in the surrounding countryside became hostile. After their bogus offer of "help" was turned down, these neighbors began a campaign of opposition. They managed to stop further progress on the temple.

It lay in ruins for nearly 20 more years, until the prophets Haggai and Zechariah (whose messages are recorded in the books named after them) again stirred up interest in building. This "second push" is described in chapters 5 and 6. When opposition arose this time, the Israelites managed to push through—again with the assistance of a Persian king.

Another problem preoccupies the final four chapters. Ezra, the man after whom this book is named, actually arrived in Jerusalem during this period, 80 years after the first party. The temple had by then been up for half a century. But the "new beginning" stood in severe jeopardy again.

The Israelites had begun to mingle (and compromise their faith) with the hostile people around them. Ezra's leadership, which came from deep biblical faith and genuine sorrow over sin, forced a radical, painful solution.

Ezra Leads Up to Jesus

The book of Ezra introduces an entirely new period in Israel's history—a period in which they became more like a church than a nation. Israelites before the exile had given much of their energy to fighting enemy armies. Now they focused on fighting sin and spiritual compromise.

The minority who returned could build a temple only with the permission of a foreign government in Persia. They had lost political independence, yet they clung to their religion, especially to the Old Testament Scriptures and temple worship. They feared repeating the mistakes that had sent them into exile. True, they did flirt with spiritual compromise. Yet when God's prophets spoke, people responded.

As those who had chosen a ruined Jerusalem over a prosperous Babylon, the returned Jews looked to God instead of to government for help. Still they dreamed, more than ever, of the powerful Messiah the prophets promised. This dream, and their strong determination to obey the law of God, continued right up until the time of Jesus, about 450 years after Ezra's last words.

How to Read Ezra

The book of Ezra describes several highly emotional events. Yet it reads like a historical report, citing official documents, letters, and lists written over an 80-year span. You are often left to imagine for yourself the feelings of the returning exiles. The book can, therefore, seem confusing and dry unless you take time to imagine how the scenes must have looked and to reflect on how people must have felt.

The three distinct periods Ezra deals with all have the same theme: a new beginning for God's people. In each situation God gave opportunity and the outside world threatened it. God's people drifted back and forth in their response. Carefully take note of the "messages" from both God and the world, and how the Israelites responded. Examine Ezra's model, as an unwavering man of the law as well as of deep personal faith.

To understand how Ezra fits into Israel's long-term pattern of response to God and the world, read some historical background. Articles on "Ezra," "Haggai" or "Israel: History of" in a Bible dictionary may offer the best summary. The short book of Haggai zeroes in on the crucial months described in Ezra 5:1-2 and makes a valuable companion to any study of Ezra.

Notes

_____

_____

_____

_____

_____

NEHEMIAH

INTRODUCTION

A Man of Action

He set out to build a wall, but left an enduring legacy of leadership

In the book of Nehemiah we peek inside the personal memoirs of a great leader. You can't mistake his style. He was an organizer, a pragmatic leader. That, no doubt, is why he had made his way to a top position in the the Persian empire, one of the grandest in the history of the world.

Yet his heart was elsewhere—in Jerusalem, a small, troublesome place far from the center of power. When he heard of the difficulties his people were experiencing there, he took his career—and probably his life—in his hands and spoke to the king about it. Shortly thereafter he was touring, by night, the broken-down walls of a city he probably had never seen before.

Nearly 100 years had passed since his people had returned to Jerusalem from exile. Though the temple had been rebuilt, the city was barely occupied. More Jews lived in the outlying villages and towns than in the holy city. They mixed with all kinds of foreigners. They were in danger of losing their identity. Why? Partly because the city lacked a wall.

What's in a Wall?

Compared to many concerns, building a wall may not seem terribly important. But think of it this way—what if the border between Mexico and the U.S. were wide open, so that anyone could cross and live on either side at will? One thing is certain: the distinction between Mexico and Texas would soon dissolve.

For lack of a wall the Jews were facing assimilation into the culture of their neighbors. In those days a city without a wall was easy pickings for any robber band. Jews, concerned for security, had scattered among other nationalities in small villages outside Jerusalem. There they were intermarrying and gradually losing their own language, culture and—most important—their own religion. A wall would give them a chance to make Jerusalem a truly Jewish city, keeping it safe and controlling who came and went.

Waiting for a Leader

What had kept them from doing anything about the broken-down wall for nearly 100 years? One obstacle was local resistance: powerful politicians were determined to keep the Jews down. Perhaps another reason was the lack of a leader like Nehemiah. In his memoirs, which fill most of this book, he shows remarkable qualities of leadership: impassioned speech, prayer, organization, resolve, trust in God, quick and determined response to problems, unselfishness. Perhaps his years in the Persian court had been preparing him. Organizing a difficult building project and handling fierce opposition seemed to come easily to him.

Nehemiah was more than a good business manager. He was a man of God. He did not act without prayer, and he did not pray without acting. His prayers punctuate the book. He recognized God's role in all that happened and never forgot to give him credit. He was not looking for earthly status—if he had been, he never would have left Persia.

How to Read Nehemiah

Nehemiah's personality is the outstanding quality of the book that bears his name. No other biblical character gives such clear information about how he "practices the presence of God" while carrying a leadership role. As you read, take note of the qualities that made Nehemiah successful as a leader and man of God. You may also wish to contrast his leadership with Ezra's. They worked in tandem but had very different styles. Nehemiah was an activist, Ezra a student; Nehemiah was outspoken, Ezra more withdrawn. Yet both faced similar problems and had similar success—and the two worked smoothly together.

The books of Ezra and Nehemiah both tell how the disgraced and chastened Jews returned from exile to rebuild their country. As history, Nehemiah includes some long lists of different family groups, as well as a detailed description of who built which parts of the Jerusalem wall. Unless you are an advanced student, you should skim these lists mainly to get an understanding of why they were kept. Concentrate more on how the Israelites had been transformed and purified by exile, making them ready to meet new challenges when they returned home.

Notes

ESTHER

INTRODUCTION

A Profile of Courage

Heroes act while others stand and watch

What makes a hero? Ask one, and you may find a surprising nonchalance: "I'm sure other people would have done exactly the same thing," they say. "I was just in the right place at the right time."

People become heroes because they take quick action at that "right time," while others stand watching in horror. The true hero recognizes the crisis and moves to meet it. This kind of courage made Esther great—worthy of a book in the Bible.

A Queen Risks Her Life

By the "accident" of her beauty and the "accident" of the former queen's dismissal, Esther found herself queen of one of the greatest powers of the world. Then, when all seemed smooth, her crucial moment came.

This moment has been echoed many times since. As a successful racial minority in the Persian empire, Esther's people, the Jews, had not melted into their surroundings. Others were jealous of their success and separatism. A vengeful prime minister, Haman, made up his mind to destroy them. He issued an edict of government-sponsored genocide.

Would Queen Esther intervene? Doing so would risk her life. And what difference could she make? She was a powerless sex partner to a king who strongly preferred women who never interfered with his wishes. She came only when he called, and he had not called her for a month. And yet she alone, of all the Jews, had access to the king.

Esther's cousin Mordecai reminded her of her unique place. "Who knows but that you have come to royal position for such a time as this?" Esther responded with action. Her courageous words are a classic statement of heroism: "I will go to the king, even though it is against the law. And if I perish, I perish" (Esther 4:16).

Coincidence or Plan?

The book of Esther shows, though indirectly, God's heroic concern for the Jews. The story runs on a series of extraordinary coincidences. Esther just "happened" to be chosen as the new queen. The king just "happened" to be unable to sleep, and when he picked up some reading, just "happened" across an account of a good deed Esther's cousin Mordecai had done. The evil Haman just "happened" along at that crucial moment. These coincidences, along with Esther's courage, tilted terrible events toward the Jews' favor.

Were these really mere coincidences? Or was God behind them? The book of Esther doesn't say directly: God is not mentioned even once, and sometimes seems deliberately left out. But believing readers, whether Jews or Christians, can have no doubt. All of life is under God's command. Nothing just happens. These coincidences were part of God's plan to save the Jews.

God protected his people because he loved them—because he had chosen them from the beginning. Even their enemies knew the "luck" of the Jews. (See Esther 6:13, for instance.) Esther's story is another chapter in the amazing story of God's perpetual love for the Jews. Though sometimes far from his will, this tiny, often hated minority has survived and thrived down the centuries.

From Haman to Hitler, vindictive leaders have hated the Jews. Yet while no other group has been so hated, no other group has shown the Jews' ability to overcome adversity. Nor can any other ethnic group alive today point to such continuity with their ancestors. They have endured as a unique and great people. How? Esther shows that God's exquisite timing—combined with the courage of individuals who "happened" to be in the right place at the right time—made his chosen people prosper.

How to Read Esther

Esther makes such suspenseful reading that most people will find it hard to quit. As in a detective story, every detail folds into another. You don't know, from one page to the next, how the drama will turn out.

The essence of Esther lies in its characters. Study Esther, Mordecai, Haman, and King Xerxes. What kind of people were they? What were their ambitions? What were their strengths and weaknesses? What crucial moment showed the true character of each? What do you learn from them that can help you rise to the challenge when you are "the right person at the right place at the right time"?

Knowing the historical setting for Esther's story can enrich your study. A good commentary or Bible dictionary (under "Esther") will illuminate many of the details that make Esther such a convincing historical document.

Notes

_____

_____

_____

_____

_____

JOB

INTRODUCTION

When Bad Things Happened to a Good Person

Nobody suffered more; nobody deserved it less

How could it happen? All at once the world came crashing down on a single innocent man, a man named Job. It was the ultimate in unfairness.

First, raiders stole his belongings and slaughtered his servants. Then fire from the sky burned up his sheep, and a mighty wind destroyed his house and killed his sons and daughters. Finally, Job came down with a horrible, painful disease. *What did I do to deserve such suffering?*, he wailed.

A Cosmic Contest

The book of Job reads like a detective story in which the readers know far more than the central characters. The very first chapter answers Job's main question: he had done nothing to deserve such suffering. We, the readers, know that, but nobody tells Job and his friends.

Unknown to him, Job was involved in a cosmic test, a contest proposed in heaven but staged on earth. In this extreme test of faith, the best man on earth suffered the worst calamaties. Satan had claimed that people like Job love God only because of the good things he provides. Remove those good things, Satan challenged, and Job's faith would melt away along with his riches and health.

God's reputation was on the line. Would Job continue to trust him, even while his life was falling apart? This is the crucial question of the book: Would Job turn against God?

Job's wife mocked him, "Are you still holding on to your integrity? Curse God and die!" (2:9). His friends were even crueler: they argued that Job was being punished, that he fully deserved the tragedies crashing into his life. For his part, Job struggled to do what seemed impossible: to keep on believing in a loving, fair God even though all the evidence pointed against such a God.

Job on Trial

It helps to think of this book as a courtroom drama, full of long, eloquent speeches. For most of the book, Job sits in the defendant's chair listening to his friends' harangues. He knows no airtight refutations; what they say about suffering as punishment seems to make sense. Yet he also knows, deep in his soul, that they are wrong. He does not deserve the treatment he is getting. There has to be some other explanation.

Like all grieving persons, Job went through emotional cycles. He whined, exploded, cajoled, and collapsed into self-pity. He agreed with his friends, then shifted positions and contradicted himself. And occasionally he came up with a statement of brilliant hope.

Mainly, Job asked for one thing: an appearance by the one Person who could explain his miserable fate. He wanted to meet God himself, face to face. Eventually Job got his wish; God did show up in person. And when God finally spoke, no one—not Job, nor any of his friends—was prepared for what he had to say.

When We Feel Like Job

Sooner or later we all find ourselves in a position somewhat like Job's. Our world seems to crumble apart. Nothing makes sense any more. God seems distant and silent.

At such moments of great crisis, each one of us is put on trial. In a sense we become actors in a contest like the one Job went through. This book records every step in that process with unflinching honesty. Job's life stands as an example to every person who must go through great suffering.

How to Read Job

The book of Job is regarded as one of the world's truly great literary masterpieces. It contains some of the finest, most expressive poetry in the Bible. Yet first-time readers of Job can easily get lost because the complete "story line" is found in the first two chapters and the last one. Everything in between consists of a series of speeches.

The boldface sectional headings and the phrases that follow, such as "And Job continued his discourse" and "Then Eliphaz the Temanite replied," serve as markers or signposts throughout the book. Rather than reading large sections of the book, read one entire speech by Job, or a speech by Job and a rebuttal from one of his friends.

It may help if you try to summarize the statement behind each speech in one sentence and write that sentence in the margin (For example, "Job protests that he's innocent"). Speakers of that day impressed their audience more by eloquence than by rigorous logic, so the speeches may seem flowery. The issues Job and his friends address, however, are life-and-death ones.

As you read the speeches of Job's friends, remember that their views do not necessarily reflect God's. The book of Job merely records the friends' viewpoints; it does not endorse them.

Notes

_____

_____

_____

_____

_____

PSALMS

INTRODUCTION

Cries from the Heart

Songs for sorrow as well as joy

Here at the very center of the Bible are songs, rising up like a tune from its heart. They capture the innermost thoughts and prayers of Old Testament people—and they still speak directly to our needs.

For every emotion and mood, you can find a psalm to match. The psalms wrestle with the deepest sorrow and ask God the hardest questions about suffering and injustice. Their voice is refreshingly spontaneous. They do not tip flowery compliments toward God: they cry out to him, or shout for joy before him.

After you read these poems, you can't think of the Old Testament as dry and rule-bound. Nor is the Old Testament God distant and impersonal. In almost every psalm you find the presence of God, not as a philosophical principle, but as an active, strong, and loving ruler—a God who makes a difference in life.

How Did the Psalms Come Together?

While almost half of the psalms are credited to David, at least one was written 500 years after his birth. A number of poets and writers contributed, and about a third of the psalms are completely anonymous.

How did the psalms come together? They seem to have been compiled as a hymnbook for use in temple worship. Some psalms were written from an individual's experiences, but were adapted for congregational use. Directions for musicians were added, along with a few verses to widen the psalms' meaning to everybody.

The psalms show tremendous variation, reflecting the many personalities who contributed their poems and prayers over several centuries. Yet readers have found an inner consistency in the whole book, so they can move from one psalm to the next without being particularly aware that one poem is centuries older than another. Some have called the psalms a Bible within the Bible— different books telling a single story.

Others have compared the book of Psalms to a beautiful cathedral built over centuries. Each wing and each window show the individual genius of its designers, yet all the parts are somehow harmonious. This harmony comes not merely from a common sense of style, but from unity of purpose: the whole cathedral is made for the worship of one and the same God. Just so, the psalms reflect, in a hundred moods and experiences, the never-changing reality of a strong and loving God, who cares for his people.

The Presence of Real Enemies

God is not the only reality in the psalms. Equally persistent are enemies who sneer and hurt and plot violence. They, too, appear in nearly every psalm. For the psalmists, faith in God was a struggle against powerful forces that often seemed more real than God.

The psalm writers frequently asked, "Where are you, God? Why don't you help me?" Despite their love of God, they often felt abandoned, misused, betrayed. They found no guarantee of safety in their closeness to God. The joy and praise that saturate these prayers came, not from an absence of problems, but from a deep conviction that a great God would overcome them.

Jesus, dying on the cross, twice expressed himself in the words of psalms (22:1 and 31:5), and his disciples, in trying to explain his life, quoted from Psalms more than any other book. They appear to have meditated on the psalms often as they considered the meaning of Jesus' life. In the psalms they could see that even the best men—even David, the great king—suffer agony and feel abandoned.

Living by faith is not easy. It was not for David; it was not for Jesus either. These powerful poems of praise and worship, some of the most beautiful ever written, offer no magical formulas to make troubles go away. Yet, while real life questions, struggles, and discouragements have a strong voice in these poems, more powerful still is the voice of joy and security in the strength and fortress of Israel: the Lord himself.

How to Read Psalms

The best way to read the psalms is also the most common way: to make these ancient prayers your own and speak them directly to God. So many of the poems catch deep human feelings that you can't help being moved by them.

But not all the psalms seem attractive. Some sound harsh, self-congratulatory, or boring. You will not find it easy to pray these until you understand them.

And there are so many psalms! This is the longest book in the Bible. To compensate, many people read only selected psalms, skimming over the others. But then they miss the deeper messages found there, including the messages that the New Testament writers saw when they quoted Psalms more than any other Old Testament book. The richest lessons from Psalms may come from particularly difficult poems you must read again and again until you begin to see what the author had in mind.

The original Hebrew of these poems probably used no rhyme or strict rhythm as traditional English poems do. Instead, the psalmists wrote with parallelism, following one thought by a "rhyming" thought or by its opposite.

Readers may be confused by the psalms' frequent change of voice. In a single poem the psalmist may talk to God, then talk about him, and then return to talking to him, all in rapid succession. This would be strange English prose, but was common in Hebrew poetry.

Because so many of the psalm titles refer to David, you may find it helpful to refer to his life story. It is found in 1 Samuel 16-31, the whole book of 2 Samuel, and the first two chapters of

1 Kings. However, most of the psalms can make perfect sense without reference to any outside information. They merely ask—and reward—time and close attention. Read and reread them. They grow richer with careful study.

Notes

_____

_____

_____

_____

PROVERBS

INTRODUCTION

Uncommon Sense

A most down-to-earth book

"Sesame Street," the educational TV show, changed a lot of people's ideas about education. It offers a kaleidoscopic mix of gentle fun that seems to have nothing to do with education at all. One episode may start with a band of puppet rock stars—the Beetles—singing an ode entitled "Letter B" (to a tune that sounds surprisingly like the Beatles' "Let It Be"). Then the picture cuts to Big Bird asking Oscar the Grouch to help him write a letter to his uncle—Uncle Bird, whose name just happens to start with the letter _B_. Five minutes later, a cartoon letter _B_ is jumping in front of various letter combinations while a voice intones the words spelled out: "B-b-boy." "B-b-bathtub." "B-b-bicycle."

"Sesame Street" showed that teaching kids doesn't always mean forcing them to sit down and memorize lists. By watching Big Bird, the Cookie Monster, and Oscar the Grouch, children painlessly learn the letter _B_ as well as colors, shapes, and a lot more.

The book of Proverbs does for wisdom what "Sesame Street" does for the ABC's. Much of Proverbs reads like a collection of one-liners, moving quickly (and apparently illogically) from one subject to another. A proverb pleases the ear much as "Sesame Street" pleases the eye, using "shortness, sense and salt" to compress life into a handful of memorable words. But just as with the TV program, Proverbs has an overall objective behind its disorder. If you spend enough time in Proverbs, you will gain a subtle and practical understanding of life.

A Father's Guidance

Proverbs is probably the most down-to-earth book in the Bible. Its education prepares you for the street and the marketplace, not the schoolroom. (Proverbs 1:20-21 expresses this poetically.) The book offers the warm advice you get by growing up in a good family: practical guidance for successfully making your way in the world. It covers small questions as well as large: talking too much, visiting neighbors too often, being unbearably cheerful too early in the morning.

The first nine chapters, which explain the purpose of Proverbs's wisdom, are spoken from father to son. Fifteen times the fatherly voice says, "My son." Some of the advice seems particularly well suited to young people: warnings against joining gangs, for instance, or urgent cautions against sex outside marriage. But the central message of Proverbs applies to anyone, old or young: "Get wisdom at all costs." It is a plea to strain your mind and your ears searching for the wise way to live.

Virtue Is Not Its Only Reward

Anybody with a brain can find exceptions to Proverbs's generalities. For instance, Proverbs 28:19 proclaims that "he who works his land will have abundant food, but the one who chases fantasies will have his fill of poverty." Yet farmers who work hard go hungry in a drought, and dreamers win $10 million in a lottery.

Proverbs simply tells how life works most of the time. You can worry about the exceptions after you have learned the rule. Try to live by the exceptions, and you court disaster.

The rule is that the godly, moral, hardworking, and wise will reap many rewards. Those who learn the practical and godly wisdom of Proverbs not only sleep better, they succeed and become able to help their family and friends. Fools and scoffers, though they appear successful, will eventually pay the cost of their lifestyle.

Much of Proverbs's practical advice makes no mention of God, and its concern for success may therefore seem quite secular. But if you take the book as a whole, it becomes obvious that the lifestyle Proverbs teaches depends on a healthy respect for God (1:7) affecting every aspect of life (3:5-7). Proverbs frankly concedes that the wise path will not be chosen by many: it is easier to live carelessly and godlessly. But those who choose to live by Proverbs will get success and safety, and more: they will get to know God himself. "Then you will understand the fear of the LORD and find the knowledge of God" (2:5).

How to Read Proverbs

People love to quote proverbs, which often express truth about life in an elegant, witty kernel. You'll find more humor in Proverbs than anywhere else in the Bible.

Yet Proverbs may well be the most abused book in the Bible. People often quote the proverbs as though they were absolute promises from God or rigid rules for living. In fact, few of the proverbs should be read that way. And some proverbs, read by themselves, would give you a distorted point of view.

To understand Proverbs, you should not hunt through it for proverbs you like. You should study the whole book to get its overall point of view. This takes time, for Proverbs covers dozens of subjects in subtle detail.

Each of the more than 500 proverbs is a tough nut you have to crack before you get the inner meat. Read Proverbs slowly, but not for too long at one sitting.

Some people like to read a small number of proverbs each day in addition to their regular Bible readings. Others concentrate on memorizing proverbs, so they can run them through their heads as they go on about the day. Whatever technique you use, keep two things in mind: think carefully about each proverb, and try to put each into the bigger context of the teachings of all of Proverbs.

The book of Proverbs is divided into two main parts: an introduction in the first nine chapters and the proverbs themselves in the remaining 22 chapters. If you skip the introduction, you won't understand the point of Proverbs as a book. It introduces "Lady Wisdom," and explains what she can do for you.

Notes

_____

_____

_____

_____

_____

ECCLESIASTES

INTRODUCTION

When Life Seems Senseless

A book for our time

"There are two tragedies in life," said George Bernard Shaw. "One is not to get your heart's desire. The other is to get it." This paradoxical proverb has often proved true. Consider a larger-than-life character from the 20th century, a man named Howard Hughes.

World's Richest Man

At age 45 Hughes was one of the most glamorous men in America. He courted actresses, piloted exotic test aircraft, and worked on top-secret CIA contracts. He owned a string of hotels around the world, and even an airline—TWA—to carry him on global jaunts.

Twenty years later, at 65, Howard Hughes still had plenty of money—$2.3 billion, to be exact. But the world's richest man had become one of its most pathetic. He lived in small, dark rooms atop his hotels, without sun and without joy. He was unkempt: a scraggly beard had grown waist-length, his hair fell well down his back, and his fingernails were two inches long. His once-powerful six-foot-four frame had shrunk to about 100 pounds.

This famous man spent most of his time watching movies over and over, with the same movie showing as many as 150 times. He lay naked in bed, deathly afraid of germs. Life held no meaning for him. Finally, emaciated and hooked on drugs, he died at age 67, for lack of a medical device his own company had helped to develop.

A King's Charmed Life

Howard Hughes is an extreme example of a syndrome that can afflict the rich and famous. His attitude toward life closely followed the thoughts of another successful man, a great king who ruled Israel long ago. This book, Ecclesiastes, records what happened to that man who had everything.

The author of Ecclesiastes had tasted just about everything life has to offer. Wealth? No one could exceed him in luxurious lifestyle (2:4-9). Wisdom? His was world-renowned (1:13-18). Fame? He was king, the most famous man of his time (1:12). Systematically, he sampled all of life's powers and pleasures, yet all ultimately disappointed him. All proved meaningless.

What is the point of life? he asked. You work hard, and someone else gets all the credit. You struggle to be good, and evil people take advantage of you. You accumulate money, and it just goes to spoiled heirs. You seek pleasure, and it turns sour on you. And everyone—rich or poor, good or evil—meets the same end. We all die. There is only one word to describe this life: meaningless!

Life Under the Sun

Ecclesiastes strikes a responsive chord in our age. Its words show up in folk songs and at presidential inaugurations. No century has seen such progress, and yet such despair. What is the purpose of life anyway? Is there any ultimate meaning? "Is that all there is?" asked one songwriter after listing life's pleasures.

A key phrase in this book, "under the sun," describes the world lived on one level, apart from God and without any belief in the afterlife. If you live on that level, you may well conclude that life is meaningless.

Ecclesiastes gives some words of hope, including the final summary: "Fear God and keep his commandments, for this is the whole duty of man" (12:13). That's the positive message, the "lesson" of Ecclesiastes. But such positive words are almost overwhelmed by the author's powerful negative example. You could summarize his whole life in Jesus' one statement, "What good will it be for a man if he gains the whole world, yet forfeits his soul?" (Matthew 16:26).

How to Read Ecclesiastes

Ecclesiastes attracts extreme reactions. For several hundred years, Jewish scholars fiercely debated whether the book should even be included in the Old Testament. Yet novelist Thomas Wolfe said of it, "Ecclesiastes is the greatest single piece of writing I have ever known, and the wisdom expressed in it the most lasting and profound."

Because of the book's unique nature, it is important to keep certain principles in mind while reading it. Consider Ecclesiastes as a whole. The Teacher was exploring various philosophies of life. During his search, he tried different approaches, including hedonism, the unrestrained pursuit of pleasure. The book honestly records the author's search without endorsing it.

At times the author concludes with despairing statements that directly contradict other parts of the Bible (for example, the recurring phrase, "Everything is meaningless!"). Read such individual statements in their context. Just as the book of Job contains arguments that God directly refuted later, so Ecclesiastes contains many isolated statements that contradict its final conclusion.

Ecclesiastes performs two very valuable functions. First, it should stimulate compassion for those who are trapped in despair and live in a meaningless world, alone, without God. The author brilliantly captures the futility and meaninglessness of that world, expressing a philosophy of life widespread in the 20th century.

But the book includes more than despair. It also blends in proverbs about how life should be lived, pungent observations that can be easily overlooked. Look for these nuggets of wisdom, especially toward the end of the book. (You may also find it helpful to balance out Ecclesiastes with the more confident advice of Proverbs.)

By asking questions, the author of Ecclesiastes helped prepare for the answers God ultimately provided. The Teacher concluded, "Everything is meaningless!" under the sun, but when Jesus Christ came he promised life "to the full" (John 10:10).

Notes

_____

_____

_____

_____

_____

SONG OF SONGS
INTRODUCTION

An Intoxicating Love
A poem about love the way it's meant to be

Snap the radio on, zip to any station, and what are you likely to hear? Love songs. Songs of new love, songs of disappointed love, songs of grateful love, songs of crazy love. Times change, but through history the flow of love songs is a constant.

Plenty of people are shocked to find an explicit love song in the Bible—complete with erotic lyrics. But Song of Songs is exactly that. It shows no embarrassment about lovers enjoying each other's bodies, and talking about it. Consequently, intermittent attempts have been made to rule Song of Songs out of the Bible or to make it for "Adults Only." In 16th-century Spain, for instance, professor Fray Luis de Leon was dragged out of his classroom and imprisoned for four years. His crime? He translated Song of Songs into Spanish.

Allegorical Interpretation

More often, Song of Songs has been read as though it had nothing to do with lovers at all. Many have interpreted it as an allegory of love between God and his people. Some of these interpretations identify every poetic detail with some corresponding facet of our relationship to God. For instance, the bride's hair may be interpreted as non-Jewish nations who come to Christ. The famous saint Bernard of Clairvaux, using this allegorical approach, wrote 86 sermons on the first two chapters of Song of Songs.

Nowadays, few follow that kind of interpretation. Most scholars believe that the poem was intended to celebrate love between a newly married couple. God values love between a man and a woman. That's why he placed this song in his holy Bible. It may have been sung first at a wedding.

Naked and Unashamed

These lovers love to look at each other. They love to tell each other what they feel. They revel in the sensuous: the beauty of nature, the scent of perfumes and spices. They are openly erotic. Their intoxication with love sounds quite up-to-date, not so different from what you hear on the radio. Yet Song of Songs conveys a very different atmosphere from most modern love songs. The explicit lyrics never become even slightly dirty. This love comes from the garden of Eden, when both man and woman were naked and unashamed. It is tender, filled with delight, natural. You sense no shame or guilt; you feel that God is with the two as they love.

The lovers act as equals. Both woman and man take the initiative in praising each other. They don't flirt or play games: they say what they mean.

Yet they show caution and dignity in their love. While at the peak of joy, the lovers repeatedly warn others not to stir up love prematurely (2:7; 3:5; 8:4). They recognize the dangerously explosive side of love. "For love is as strong as death, its jealousy unyielding as the grave. It burns like blazing fire, like a mighty flame" (8:6).

How to Read Song of Songs

Since love songs are always popular, many people approach Song of Songs with great expectations. However, readers often find the book different from what they had expected.

Two main problems may hinder today's reader. One is the poetic imagery. No modern lover would say, "Your hair is like a flock of goats" (4:1), or, "Your nose is like the tower of Lebanon" (7:4). While some images in Song of Songs appeal—"His banner over me is love" (2:4) or "Love is as strong as death" (8:6)—the majority of the book's metaphors sound strange to our ears.

Most of the comparisons aren't visual, but emotional. For instance, when the lover tells his beloved that "your two breasts are like two fawns," he isn't saying that her breasts look like deer. He is saying that they bring out the same tender feelings baby deer do. When you read strange-sounding metaphors in Song of Songs, don't ask, "What did these things (pomegranates, myrrh, a flock of sheep) look like?" but ask, "What did the lovers *feel* when they thought of them?"

A second problem: Song of Songs is hard to follow. One part doesn't seem connected to the next. Think of it as a series of snapshots of a couple in love—snapshots not necessarily in order. Put together in one photo album, they show the profound feelings of newly married lovers.

Though Song of Songs is primarily about love on the human level, many Christians and Jews have read it as a book about God's love. This was probably not the author's original intent, but it is a legitimate and inspiring way to look at the book. After all, God made human love, and other parts of the Bible suggest its similarity to God's love. (See Hosea 1-3 and Ephesians 5:22-33.) Song of Songs never makes this connection, but it does present a love so rich, so full, so unashamed that it's natural to think of God and his love for us.

Notes

_____

_____

_____

_____

_____

ISAIAH

INTRODUCTION

Prophet, Poet, and Politician

His nation at a crossroads, Isaiah rose to meet the challenge

The prophet Isaiah was a giant of Jewish history. He was the Shakespeare of Hebrew literature, and the New Testament quotes him more than all the other prophets combined. No other biblical author can match his rich vocabulary and use of imagery.

And yet Isaiah spent his days not in an ivory tower, but in the corridors of power. He served as adviser to the kings of Judah and helped set the course of his nation.

Days of Crisis

Isaiah lived at a crucial time, midway between the founding of the kingdom under Saul and David and its eventual destruction. A civil war had split the Israelites into North (Israel) and South (Judah), and Isaiah lived in the more pious Southern Kingdom.

When Isaiah began his work, the nation seemed strong and wealthy. But Isaiah saw signs of grave danger. People were using their power to harass the poor. Men went around drunk; women cared more about their clothes than about their neighbors' hunger. People gave lip service to God and kept up the outward appearance of religion but did little more.

Outside dangers loomed even larger. The armies of neighboring Israel were rattling swords and spears at the border. On all sides, monster empires were growing, especially Egypt and Assyria. Judah was caught in a pincers. Should the nation choose one of the empires as an ally?

Harsh Words from an Uncompromising Prophet

The nation of Judah, said Isaiah, stood at a crossroads: it could either regain its footing or begin a dangerous slide downward. The prophet did not temper his message for the sake of popular opinion. He had harsh and unyielding words about what changes must take place.

Although he moved in royal circles, Isaiah was hardly a yes-man in politics. Sometimes he stood alone against a tide of optimism. His very name meant "The Lord saves," and he warned kings that relying on military power or wealth or any force other than God would lead to disaster.

Isaiah outlasted four kings, but he finally offended one beyond repair. King Manasseh (notorious for practicing infant sacrifice) found Isaiah's strong words too much to bear. Tradition records that he had Isaiah killed by fastening him between two planks of wood and sawing his body in half.

Manasseh has long since disappeared into obscurity. But Isaiah, through this book, endures as one of the great authors of all time. Sometimes the pen *is* mightier than the sword.

How to Read Isaiah

In the eighth century B.C., about the time Homer was writing *The Iliad* and *The Odyssey*, Isaiah wrote the book that bears his name. It is arguably the most eloquent book in the Old Testament, and you will likely recognize many verses and phrases.

Isaiah is full of profound insights into the nature of God and his plan for the earth. Due to its length and its peculiar organization, however, the book may seem hard to grasp.

Remember that Isaiah consists of a collection of many messages on various topics, pulled together into groupings. To understand Isaiah, it helps to think of "road markers" that set off the major groupings. Here is a summary of them:

Isaiah 1-12: Isaiah's call and messages of warning to Judah during the prosperous days of the kingdom.

Isaiah 13-23: Isaiah's messages to all the nations around Judah—including enemies and close allies.

Isaiah 24-35: A view of the earth's future (24-27) and specific messages to the people of Judah as they faced Assyria's imminent invasion.

Isaiah 36-39: An interlude telling of great crises faced by King Hezekiah. The focus of the book moves from Assyria to Babylon.

Isaiah 40-48: Prophecies addressed to a very different situation, 200 years into the future. Now Babylon, not Assyria, is the great enemy.

Isaiah 49-55: A word of hope about final deliverance through the "suffering servant."

Isaiah 56-66: General warnings to Judah, and a view of the future.

Notes

_____

_____

_____

_____

_____

JEREMIAH

INTRODUCTION

God's Reluctant Messenger

Jeremiah felt frightened and insecure—but he burned with a message

Jeremiah lived one of the most dramatic lives in the Bible, and that is saying something. But he never learned to like his role. Through all the excitement he remained reluctant, insecure, and often unhappy.

God chose him to be "over nations and kingdoms to uproot and tear down, to destroy and overthrow, to build and to plant" (1:10). To accomplish that, Jeremiah had only one resource, his mouth. How did he respond to such an awesome challenge? "Ah, Sovereign LORD," he said, "I do not know how to speak; I am only a child" (1:6). He didn't stride forward; he barely hung on. He wanted out of the job.

His only encouragement was God's promise: "Today I have made you a fortified city, an iron pillar and a bronze wall to stand against the whole land" (1:18). For 40 years Jeremiah gave top officials a warning they hated to hear and refused to heed. Several times they arrested and imprisoned him; they nearly killed him.

His message? With God's approval, the savage Babylonians would sweep down into Judah. Clever alliances with other powers like Egypt would not help, said Jeremiah. Neither would Judah's half-hearted religion. Judah's only hope lay in renewing an alliance with the living God.

A Disturbing Glimpse of Jeremiah's Mind

The book of Jeremiah stands out not for beautiful poetry or great ideas. Its power comes from its disturbing glimpse of Jeremiah's mind. Jeremiah talked like a man who has awakened from a nightmare, convinced that the nightmare is coming true. His words were sledgehammer blows designed to crack the hardest, most indifferent skull. Though he wished to keep quiet, he found that God's "word is in my heart like a fire, a fire shut up in my bones" (20:9).

No prophet exposed his feelings more than Jeremiah. His relationship with God was streaked with quarrels, reproaches, and outbursts. He told God he wished he were dead (20:14-18). He accused God of being unreliable (15:18). But God offered no sympathy. Rather, he promised more of the same, reminding Jeremiah of his promise to stand by him (12:5-6; 15:19-20). Their relationship, doubts and all, forms one of the best examples in the Bible of what it means to follow God in spite of everything.

Reason to Fear

Jeremiah frankly feared death. He wearied of ridicule. He hated standing alone against the crowd. He told God how he felt. Yet he obeyed God, and in the end his message proved true. He stands as a far greater man than the kings in their luxurious palaces who imprisoned him and burned his writings.

He spoke a gloomy message in a gloomy time, and as a result his words are not always pleasant to read. He reminds us, in an era of artificial cheer and television smiles, that God's message is not always comforting and encouraging. People who disregard him will have reason to fear. For a world that defies him, he plans judgment. And no one, not even his chosen messengers, will escape suffering. God's presence will make them strong enough to face it.

How to Read Jeremiah

Suppose you find, in an old trunk, a thick packet of letters written by your great uncle. You soon realize they are all out of order. One he wrote from the trenches of France during World War I. The next also refers to a war, but from the references to Winston Churchill you soon recognize it as World War II, over 20 years later.

Those letters might contain the whole of your uncle's life, but to get his story straight, you'd have to read the whole packet. A reader of Jeremiah finds a very similar situation. The book is an anthology of prophecies given at different times. They jump forward and backward in history, and if you imagine that the book is in chronological order, you will become very confused. Fortunately, it is not hard to reconstruct the order of the main events of Jeremiah's life.

Jeremiah spoke to a nation about to be destroyed by war. Three hundred years before him, the Israelites had split into two countries, Israel in the North and Judah in the South. About 100 years before Jeremiah, Assyria had conquered the Northern Kingdom. This disaster was "World War I" in Old Testament history.

Now, during Jeremiah's life, World War II threatened. Another fierce kingdom, Babylon, assembled troops against the remaining Southern Kingdom. Would God save his chosen people? Jeremiah loudly insisted for more than 20 years that God would punish Judah just as he had Israel, by letting Babylon take them into captivity. He lived to see his predictions come true.

Many passages in Jeremiah refer to the five kings he knew. When you see their names, use them as a reference point in figuring out the order of events:

Josiah (17 years)
Jehoahaz (3 months)
Jehoiakim (12 years)
Jehoiachin (3 months)
Zedekiah (11 years)

To capture the full emotion of Jeremiah, you may want to read the first few chapters out loud.

Notes

_____

_____

_____

_____

_____

LAMENTATIONS

INTRODUCTION

A City in Ruins

There was nothing left to do but weep

Every year the world pauses to remember one awful day in Hiroshima, when the power of the atom came out of the sky. Opinions vary over whether an atom bomb was necessary to end World War II. Necessary or not, however, Hiroshima was a horrible tragedy. Though the survivors have gone on with their lives, they cannot forget. Nor can the rest of the world. Hiroshima's shadow stretches down to our time.

Five Poems of Grief

Lamentations offers five poems written from a state of dazed grief worthy of Hiroshima. A whole city has been destroyed. Brothers, sisters, children, friends are all gone. Men the town admired wander the body-littered streets, their skins shriveled and their faces barely recognizable. Starvation has even compelled women to cook their own children (4:10).

And so the author mourns. He carefully reviews everything he has seen and felt, his pain darkening every line. He writes the first four poems in an acrostic style, following the Hebrew alphabet, one letter for each stanza. Perhaps this system helps him to pursue the subject thoroughly, and not to break down in spasms of emotion. When he thinks of the starving children, he nearly does (2:11).

God Caused the Carnage

The author of Lamentations—perhaps Jeremiah—evidently had seen the siege and destruction of Jerusalem in 586 B.C., when the Babylonian army burned and destroyed all the principal buildings and carried most of the surviving inhabitants into exile. Lamentations conducts a kind of post mortem on the death of Jerusalem, examining the body in clinical detail.

Like a doctor, Lamentations's author seeks to know the cause of death. He has no final doubt: though the Babylonians did the work, ultimately God was responsible. But could God willingly create such misery? The author seems stunned that God has actually destroyed his own people, though he admits they richly deserved the punishment. "The Lord is like an enemy," he cries in astonishment (2:5). "Even when I call out or cry for help, he shuts out my prayer" (3:8). "He dragged me from the path and mangled me and left me without help" (3:11). "He has broken my teeth with gravel" (3:16).

But, though astonished and grief-stricken, the author never doubts God's justice. Jerusalem's destruction came as a result of sin (1:5). This fact prompts quiet hope, based on the character of God. "Though he brings grief, he will show compassion, so great is his unfailing love. For he does not willingly bring affliction or grief to the children of men" (3:32-33). When sin is eliminated the Lord acts quickly to forgive and heal.

Looking for Recovery

Though the grief of Lamentations is as deep and heavy as any ever written, hope lies at the bottom. The author does not say "Cheer up!" to himself or anyone else. He mourns passionately and fully. But in mourning he looks to recovery. Lamentations ends with a prayer to God, asking him to restore his people, "unless you have utterly rejected us and are angry with us beyond measure" (5:22). Behind that "unless" lies confidence. God can never be angry without limits.

The author of Lamentations doesn't soften his words to God, for fear of offending him. He expresses the full and dreadful horror of what he has seen, and he gives God full responsibility. But, remembering that the Lord is a loving God, he counts on God to heal Israel's wounds. This time of mourning will be followed by another time, a time to dance.

How to Read Lamentations

Lamentations is poetry, one poem per chapter. Its main purpose is not to describe events, nor to teach lessons, though it does both. Its intent is to express grief, to pour out before God the horror and bitterness of what has happened to Jerusalem. These five poems can help you to understand what it meant for Jews to see Jerusalem destroyed. They can also help you learn to deal appropriately with grief, your own or others'. Read them expressively, preferably out loud, so that you catch the deep emotion. Note that the author does not rush to express his hope in God, but fully grieves for the tragedy he was involved in.

Lamentations is not difficult to understand, though some of the poetical allusions may become clearer if you use a Bible dictionary or a commentary. For a summary of the destruction that inspired Lamentations, read 2 Kings 25.

Notes

_____

_____

_____

_____

_____

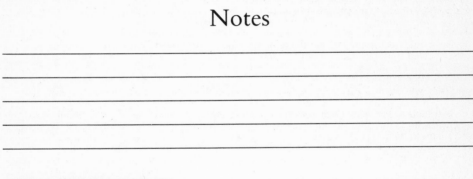

EZEKIEL

INTRODUCTION

Seeing the Unseen God

God showed himself to Ezekiel in unearthly radiance

Ezekiel begins with a description so unearthly that some have suggested the prophet saw a UFO. Indeed, there are similarities: glowing lights, quick movements, inhuman figures shrouded with fire. But at least one critical difference sets Ezekiel's story apart. UFOs typically appear in remote places and then mysteriously zoom off, never to be heard from again. The majestic being Ezekiel described was not rushing off to disappear. He wanted to be known—by everyone.

For Ezekiel was quite sure that he had seen and heard the God of the Bible. While few have been privileged to see him as Ezekiel did, this God had been speaking plainly for generations. His words were on record.

Before such splendor Ezekiel felt utterly weak and inadequate, just as Isaiah had during a similar vision (Isaiah 6). He fell on his face, repeatedly. But God raised Ezekiel to his feet and gave him a message to deliver.

A Stunning Portrait of God

In describing his call by God, Ezekiel groped for words. He portrayed a God of stunning grandeur, above and beyond our world. Yet this supernatural God was inescapably near and real. He demanded complete obedience. Surprisingly, he appeared to Ezekiel in Babylon—the last place an Israelite expected to see him. This God could not be locked in by national or geographical boxes. He ruled the earth.

Ezekiel repeated this classic message over 60 times: "Then they will know that I am the LORD." God said it when promising the destruction of Jerusalem in the first 24 chapters. He said it when predicting the downfall of Israel's neighbors in chapters 25 through 32. And, after Jerusalem had fallen, God said it when promising a great future in the last 16 chapters. God did not want to remain vague or far off. He wanted his people to know him. More, Ezekiel's God wanted to live with his people. He wanted to make his home in the center of their city.

A Strange Book

Ezekiel has a reputation for strangeness, partly because of the unearthly visions with which his book begins and ends, and partly because Ezekiel acted out God's messages through some bizarre behavior. (For instance, for months at a time he lay in public on his side, bound by ropes, facing a clay model of Jerusalem.) Strange? When a car is driving over the edge of a cliff, you may take strange measures to get the driver's attention. You may scream and gesture so wildly people think you are insane. So it was with Ezekiel. His message came in the most vivid form possible, meant to force people to pay attention.

Ezekiel lived in perhaps the most tragic period of his people's existence. They had been tempting fate for generations, ignoring God's messengers (prophets like Micah, Amos, Isaiah) who warned that if they didn't listen to God, they would be destroyed. Finally, Babylonian armies swept through Judah, deporting large groups of citizens.

Ezekiel had gone into exile in one of the first groups, as had Daniel. Ezekiel became God's messenger as a captive in Babylon. His voice blended in stereo with Jeremiah's, still in Jerusalem. Both prophets warned their people (who kept plotting ways to break free of Babylon) that the captives were going to be in Babylon for a long time. They predicted that Babylon's oppression would grow heavier: Jerusalem and the temple would be destroyed. Since Judah had ignored God's repeated warnings, God would use another means to get their attention: suffering.

A New Jerusalem

Yet even while punishing them, God's aim remained the same: to make himself known. God had warned Ezekiel that the Israelites were unlikely to listen (3:7), even from captivity. They preferred idols to the living God. Yet Ezekiel's messages and dramas and visions continued to come, year after year. It's as though God were saying through him, "Some way, some day, I will get through to them. If the message doesn't reach their hearts one way, I'll try another."

Ezekiel ends with hope. The final chapters show a new Jerusalem rising from the ruins of the old. The renewed city would never die, for it would be built on an unshifting reality: "They will know I am the LORD." The burning vision of God that Ezekiel had seen would become accessible to all. God would make himself at home there forever. Ezekiel's last verse says it all: "And the name of the city from that time on will be: THE LORD IS THERE."

How to Read Ezekiel

The special difficulty in reading Ezekiel is the dizzying variety of forms he used to get his message across. The book is like a multimedia package—a mix of visions, messages, dramas, poems. But three remarkable visions of God bracket the package, beginning, middle, and end (1:1–3:15; 8:1-6 and 11:16-25; 40:1-4 and 43:1-9). And throughout, one line is repeated: "Then they will know that I am the LORD." All God's messages are meant to shock his people into restoring a living relationship with him.

As you read Ezekiel, note down when each prophecy was made and its dominant image—Jerusalem as a prostitute, as a spreading grapevine, as a shaved head, etc. Don't skip ahead too fast as you read—take time to think about the message in each section. Remember that the book of Ezekiel compresses messages God gave over 22 years. Try to imagine the impact of each message on the people who first heard or saw it.

Most of what Ezekiel said in Babylonia concerned a dramatic military situation hundreds of miles away in Jerusalem. His message changed from doom to hope in chapter 33; the turning point came with news of Jerusalem's fall. You can get to know the historical situation by reading 2 Kings 23:36–25:12.

A fascinating though difficult study is the design of the renewed temple, which Ezekiel described in chapters 40-43. A commentary on Ezekiel or a Bible dictionary (under "Ezekiel" or "temple") can help immensely in understanding these visions.

Notes

"Kidnapped"

Even as prime minister, Daniel remained a lonely outsider

As a young man, Daniel could have anticipated an outstanding future in Jerusalem. He came from a prominent family, and he had a first-rate mind (1:4). But, when the Babylonian army dragged him captive to a faraway country, they didn't ask about his plans and dreams.

True, the Babylonians recognized Daniel's potential and put him into a top civil service training program. But even the study material was distasteful to a Jew: it covered sorcery, magic, and a pagan, multigod religion. After graduation Daniel was put to work for the Babylonian king, who continued to war against Daniel's people for nearly 20 more years.

Anyone far from home feels lonely. But Daniel was one of those whose lives get lost in the shuffle of history—refugees, captives. He was destined to spend his life as an alien in Babylon. We have no record that he ever married or had family members nearby.

Great Personal Courage

Through his ability and God's blessing he rose to the post of prime minister of Babylon. Yet he remained an outsider. The higher he rose, the more prominent a target he became. Babylonians resented his foreign background and his political success. Their plots put him under pressure to compromise his faith, to fit in, to bend his principles. His life was often at risk.

Daniel's career near the top lasted at least 66 years, so that by the time he was thrown into the lions' den (chapter 6), he must have been in his 80s. Throughout these years he labored with great effectiveness for Babylon. He was respectful and diligent, even though working for pagan kings. Yet he never compromised his faith. He would not bend, even when threatened with death. The Bible offers no better model of how to live with and serve people who do not share or respect your beliefs.

The Shape of the Future

Near the end of Daniel's life God gave him a series of visions, described in chapters 7-12. In graphic images God showed Daniel the pattern of future history. Daniel's people would duplicate his own experience, but on a world stage.

The Jews, Daniel's visions showed, would be caught in a political storm, battered about by a series of world empires. Daniel foresaw nations raging in battle against each other. He foresaw God's people thrown in between these nations, suffering through no fault of their own. They would be helpless until God himself rescued them from their troubles. Daniel foresaw, in the end, all people falling down to worship "one like a son of man." This was the title Jesus applied to himself when he came, nearly a thousand years after Daniel, to bring the good news of salvation for all people.

Spreading the Word

Daniel's people had thought of God in terms of their own small community, their own capital city and the temple there. Not only were the Jews God's chosen people, but (they tended to think) they held exclusive rights to him.

But God had never intended his blessings to stop with the Jews. He had the world in mind. At the time he called Abraham, he had promised that through Abraham's offspring he would bless the whole earth (Genesis 12:3).

The Jews had found it difficult enough to keep their own faith, let alone spread it to others. Only while captives in Babylon, unwillingly dragged far from home, did they begin to convince others that their God deserved honor. The proclamations Nebuchadnezzar and Darius made because of Daniel (4:2-3; 6:26-27) honored God more than anything a king of Judah had done in years.

How to Read Daniel

Daniel breaks into two parts, each quite different from the other. The first six chapters tell the "famous" Daniel stories—including the stories of three men thrown into a fiery furnace and Daniel in the lions' den. Any of these chapters would make a script for a thriller. As you read them, reflect on the principles Daniel lived by, far from home and in dangerous circumstances. Ask yourself what Daniel can teach you about faithfulness to God in similarly "alien" circumstances.

Most people find chapters 7-12 far more difficult: they record Daniel's visions about the future of world history. Such symbolism was a familiar mode of expression in the ancient world, but it reads very strangely now—almost like science fiction. Look for broad impressions of how God's people can live, caught in the jaws of brutal world politics. Let the visual symbols engage your emotions and imagination.

If you seek a more detailed understanding of these visions, a commentary on Daniel will be a great help. In some passages, background information on ancient world history is essential. A good commentary can offer this, along with an interpretation of difficult symbols.

Notes

_____

_____

_____

_____

_____

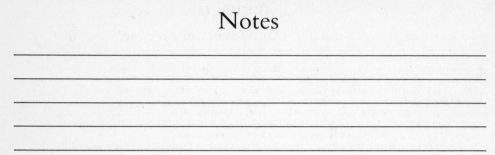

HOSEA

INTRODUCTION

Tearing God's Heart

Why would he love such a woman?

Hosea begins with a love story—a painful, personal love story, the prophet's very own. Hosea had married a woman who acted like a prostitute. Yet the more she went out on him, the more Hosea loved her. He gave her everything a good wife deserved: his love, his home, his name, his reputation. She responded by shacking up with other men. He warned her, he pleaded with her, he punished her. She humiliated him until he wanted to cry, yet still he clung to her.

Why did Hosea begin with his personal life? Because God had expressly told him to relate it to another, more tragic love story: the painful love of God for his people. God could have simply declared, "Israel is like a wife to me—an adulterous wife." Instead, he used Hosea to act out the treachery in real life—and to show in living color God's fury, his jealousy, and above all else, his love for his people.

Winding Down to a Bitter End

Virtually every chapter of Hosea talks about the "prostitution" or "adultery" of God's people (1:2; 2:2,4; 3:1; 4:2,10-15,18; 5:3,4; 6:10; 7:4; 8:9; 9:1). Underlying some hard words is a remarkably tender revelation: God doesn't want to be only "master" to his people. He wants to be a husband, giving all of himself in intimate love.

Hosea spoke and acted these messages to the Northern part of God's divided country—Israel or "Ephraim," as Hosea called it. King Jeroboam II's reign was a time of prosperity; the prophet Amos blasted the rich for their greedy injustices toward the poor. But soon after Jeroboam's death the national fabric began to unravel. In just over 20 years six kings took the throne—four of them by murdering the previous king. Hosea probably lived to see the massive Assyrian armies storm the capital and deport all the Israelite citizens to other lands. God's "wife" was carried off, just as he had warned.

God Is a Lover

When most people must have been preoccupied with politics and military matters, Hosea kept his message aimed at idol worship, which he referred to as adultery. He saw that as the root of Israel's problems.

Israel tended to mix religions freely—to think that everybody's religion had a little truth in it, and the more religion you got, the better off you would be. Many prophets attacked Israel's idol worship. Hosea shows that God's concern about idolatry is no fussy, religious matter. It is terribly personal. God, the lover, will not share his bride with anyone else.

God's anger and jealousy, expressed so often throughout the Old Testament, reflect his powerful love. Sin does not merely break God's law, it breaks his heart. He punishes to get his lover's attention. Yet even when she turns her back on him, he sticks with her. He is willing to suffer, in hope that someday she will change. Hosea shows that God longs not to punish, but to love.

How to Read Hosea

Hosea is one of the most emotional books in the Bible, an outpouring of suffering love from God's heart. This shows in the writing, which jumps impulsively from one thought to the next. Read a chapter dramatically aloud, and you will get this sense. It is almost like listening in on a husband-and-wife fight.

The book divides into two parts. In the first three chapters, the prophet Hosea briefly describes his marriage to an adulterous woman and makes the connection to Israel's unfaithfulness to God. From chapter 4 onward this dramatic, personal beginning is not mentioned again. But it has set the stage. God's deep love, his disappointment and anger, and his determination to persevere with his unfaithful wife pour out in a series of vivid speeches.

For a historical perspective on Hosea's times, read from 2 Kings 14:23 to 17:41, noting that some sections describe Judah, the Southern nation, while the rest relate to the deteriorating Israel Hosea knew. The prophet Amos spoke to the North at about the same time as Hosea, but from a noticeably different point of view. Amos concentrated on law and justice, with special concern for the poor, while Hosea concentrated on the broken relationship with God that led to this injustice. Together, these two prophets provide a three-dimensional view of Israel's problems.

Because Hosea is so emotional, he doesn't stop to explain a large number of images or biblical references. A Bible dictionary will help you understand the names and places you aren't familiar with.

Notes

_____

_____

_____

_____

_____

JOEL

INTRODUCTION

The Meaning of a Natural Disaster
What's behind a devastating locust plague?

"Their number was astounding; the whole face of the mountain was black with them. On they came like a living deluge. We dug trenches, and kindled fires, and beat and burned to death 'heaps upon heaps'; but the effort was utterly useless. Wave after wave rolled up the mountainside and poured over rocks, walls, ditches and hedges—those behind covering up and bridging over the masses already killed. It was perfectly appalling to watch this animated river as it flowed up the road, and ascended the hill above my house. For four days they continued to pass on toward the east. . . .''

W. M. Thomson is describing a locust plague. Descriptions of the aftermath sound just as awful. When locusts have passed, the terrain looks as though it has been swept by a scorching fire.

Why Have I Lived?

Many awestruck observers have written accounts of locust swarms, but none more graphically than the prophet Joel. In striking, polished imagery he described the devastation. His people faced starvation. Joel drew a verbal portrait of grief and fear.

Natural disasters provoke questions. Why did God allow this disaster to happen? Why have I lived and others died? Is there a lesson here? For Joel, a plague of locusts led to deep insights into God's universal plan.

Joel had no doubt that God was behind the plague. In fact, he pictured God leading the locusts like an army into battle (2:11). They represented "the day of the LORD," judgment on Israel. Unlike many of the other prophets, Joel did not devote time to an analysis of Israel's failings. He concentrated, instead, on a cure.

Joel urged the priests to call a nationwide day of prayer and fasting to lead the people back to God. Then God would roll back the damage done by the locusts, and more: "You will have plenty to eat, until you are full, and you will praise the name of the LORD your God, who has worked wonders for you" (2:26). They would emerge from the experience with new, durable confidence in God's love. So it has often proved for God's people: a disaster has pressed them to a deeper relationship with him.

God's Bigger Plans

Though the locust plague was by far the worst Joel had ever heard of (1:2-3), no historical record of this particular invasion has endured, other than the one Joel left us. The truth is, even the worst natural disasters fade from memory. Joel wanted the disaster to turn people's attention toward something more lasting—to an eternal God.

Joel wanted God's people to believe that God controlled the locusts, and even more importantly, that God shaped the entire course of history to his plan. As terribly as the locusts had destroyed, and as wonderfully as God had rolled back their destruction, these events only foreshadowed far more terrible and wonderful things. Joel saw that God's Spirit would transform his people into those who love him constantly, not just when a disaster catches their attention. After a time of terrible judgment, God would create a renewed, secure city for his people, in which he himself would live.

How to Read Joel

Joel breaks naturally into two parts. Up to 2:28, it talks about a locust invasion and the response of God's people to such a natural disaster. From that verse on, however, Joel's view rises above the local situation and deals with the far-off future.

Joel rarely refers to unfamiliar people, places, or events, so you can read it fairly easily without using any outside reference like a Bible dictionary. The challenge is to connect his understanding of a natural disaster—a locust plague—with his vision of the future.

The Bible often refers to "the day of the LORD" as the time when God will completely take charge of our world. But Joel seems to see "the day of the LORD" partly revealed in the disasters of his day. As you read, try to see the similarities Joel draws between the locust invasion and the final consummation of history. Ask yourself: how do I respond to disaster? How would Joel want me to respond?

Notes

_____

_____

_____

_____

_____

AMOS

INTRODUCTION

Justice!

A simple farmer takes on a materialistic nation

Business had never been better. For the first time in generations, Israel faced no military threat. Since they controlled the crucial trade routes, merchants piled up big profits. Luxuries became readily available—new stone houses, ivory-inlaid furniture, top-grade meat and fine wine, the best body lotions.

Amid such peace and prosperity, one lone voice scraped like fingernails on a blackboard. Amos spoke bluntly with a farmer's vocabulary, calling the city socialites "cows" (4:1). A mere shepherd—among the poorest of all professions—he treated luxury with scorn. Worst of all, Amos was a foreigner from the South—from Tekoa, a small town in Judah. Since Israel had split from the South about 170 years before, Israelite leaders did not take kindly to criticism from a Southerner.

But to Amos, social acceptance didn't matter. He was no professional prophet, making his living talking smoothly about God (7:14). God had called him to leave his job and carry a message. God had said go, and Amos had obeyed.

God's View of "Religion"

The people Amos addressed had plenty of "religion." They went regularly to shrines for worship. They looked forward to "the day of the LORD," when God would fulfill all their expectations for their country. But Amos brought unexpected bad news from God: "I hate, I despise your religious feasts . . . " (5:21). God didn't want sacrifice or singing. He demanded justice.

Amos listed all Israel's neighbors, announcing God's judgment for their crimes against humanity. Israelites liked this kind of talk; they felt superior to all these nations. But having caught the Israelites' attention, Amos circled dramatically home. God would judge Israel too. The people, their beautiful homes, their sacred altars—all would be destroyed.

The Character of God

More than any other book in the Bible, Amos concentrates on injustice. Israel had plenty of other faults he might have blasted. Their religious system, for instance, centered on two calf-idols. But Amos wasted little breath on that. He focused on the facts that met his eyes and ears in every marketplace: oppression of the poor, dishonest business, bribery in court, privilege bought with money.

The wealthy Israelites were getting their luxuries at the expense of the poor. They congratulated themselves on their devotion to God with no sense that they had cut the heart out of their relationship to him. They wanted God to fit conveniently into life as an additive. God showed himself through Amos as lordly, absolute, inescapable. He must be master over all of life, including business affairs.

How to Read Amos

Perhaps because he was a farmer, Amos used a plain writing style, filled with strong country language. The organization of his book is clear too: chapters 1-2 line up the Middle Eastern nations for trial, chapters 3-6 give a series of messages from God (usually beginning with "Hear this word"), and the last three chapters convey God's judgment through five graphic visions.

Throughout, Amos sticks close to his main concern: cruelty and inhumanity between people. The injustices Amos condemns often sound familiar today. As you read, ask yourself, "What would Amos say about me and about my people?"

It is a good idea to read Amos and Hosea together, for they give two views of the same situation. A visitor from the South, Amos was shocked by the injustices he saw in every marketplace. Hosea emphasized the inner dimension, an abused relationship to a loving God.

Amos predicted that Israel would be punished, and his prediction proved right. After King Jeroboam, the government deteriorated. Five kings took the throne in the next 13 years; four were assassinated. In 30 years Israel was permanently dismantled by Assyrian armies. For historical background, read 2 Kings 14:23–17:41, noting that the kings of both Israel and Judah are interspersed.

Notes

_____

_____

_____

_____

_____

OBADIAH

INTRODUCTION

Poetic Justice

Obadiah gave the final word on a blood feud

The feud began with twin brothers, Jacob and Esau. Esau, the older by minutes, would have inherited family leadership, but in a moment of hunger he traded it for a meal (Genesis 25:19-34). Jacob went on to become the founding father of the nation of Israel. Esau, a born hunter, moved southeast to desolate mountain country. He founded the nation of Edom.

Their descendants continued the quarrel. Over hundreds of years the two nations battled repeatedly but inconclusively. The Edomites' capital, Sela, sat on a high plateau above a sheer cliff: the only access was by a deep ravine. From that well-protected enclave, the Edomites raided Israel.

Though the Israelites had been commanded, "Do not abhor an Edomite, for he is your brother" (Deuteronomy 23:7), they grew to regard the Edomites as cruel and heartless. Repeatedly the prophets predicted Edom's punishment by God. The final straw came when Babylon dismembered Jerusalem and took its citizens into exile. The Edomites egged on the conquering army, preyed on fleeing Israelites, and helped plunder Jerusalem. Psalm 137, one of the saddest passages in the Bible, records the Israelite bitterness over this. As Esau had cared more for a meal than for the family name, so his descendants cared more for the profit they could get from plunder than for the compassion they owed a brother.

Fair Return for Cruelty

Obadiah predicts poetic justice for proud Edom: their treachery toward Judah (verses 11-12) repaid with treachery from their own allies (7), their robbery (13) repaid with robbery (5-6), their violence (10) with violence (9), their love of destruction (12-14) repaid with utter destruction (10,18). Obadiah predicts that downtrodden Israel will rise again, while Edom will disappear from the face of the earth.

This prediction came precisely true. Edom was destroyed, not by Israel, but by a series of foreign invaders. The last remnant of Edomites were destroyed in the Roman siege of Jerusalem in 70 A.D. Ironically, the nation that had tormented Jews in Jerusalem later died defending that city.

Why does this blood feud earn a place in Scripture? It demonstrates God's ongoing protection of his people from their enemies. It also shows that God's standards extend beyond his chosen people. Every nation will be judged, like Edom, by their own standard: "As you have done, it will be done to you" (15).

How to Read Obadiah

The shortest book in the Old Testament, Obadiah can easily be read and understood in one sitting. Many readers, however, have a hard time seeing the importance of this ongoing border feud between blood relatives.

A Bible dictionary can summarize the centuries of violence. Look under "Edom." Perhaps, though, you can only fully appreciate Israel's feelings by reflecting on your own when a close relative treats you cruelly. A family betrayal is uniquely offensive to God and humanity. Obadiah reminds us that justice will be done.

Notes

_____

_____

_____

_____

_____

INTRODUCTION

Good News for the Enemy?
Jonah balked at loving the cruel Assyrians

Jesus told his followers, "Love your enemies and pray for those who persecute you" (Matthew 5:44). While everyone talks admiringly about that command, loving your enemies is no easy thing. Many people doubt whether it is even right. Should we forgive the Nazis? Should we make a point to be kind to the Ku Klux Klan?

The book of Jonah tells the story of a man whom God instructed to love his enemies in Nineveh. True to life, the prophet Jonah did just the opposite of what God commanded. He refused to go to the people he hated. Instead, he tried to run away from the Lord.

Nineveh was a large, important city in Assyria, situated on the river Tigris. It posed a grave military threat to tiny Israel. God sent Jonah there, and he responded without hesitation: in Joppa he caught a boat going in the opposite direction. Obviously, Jonah didn't want to warn Nineveh's citizens they were about to be destroyed. He suspected they would repent and God would forgive them.

Why Jonah Didn't Want to Go

We can't be sure why Jonah hated Assyria, but another short Old Testament book, Nahum, gives a clue. This book, also completely dedicated to Nineveh, describes a ruthless, bloodthirsty people. The Assyrians themselves left monuments to their cruelty—long, boastful inscriptions describing their torture and slaughter of people who opposed them.

Israelites had reasons to hate and fear Nineveh. But God *loved* Nineveh. He wanted to save the city, not destroy it. He knew Nineveh was ripe for change. When Jonah finally preached there, the entire city believed his message and repented. Though cruel and hardened, Nineveh was ready to believe God. Israel had never responded to a prophet like these Assyrians did.

An Attitude Like God's

Since God repeatedly warned the Jews not to intermarry with people of other religions, and even ordered them to drive other nations out of the promised land, some readers conclude that the Old Testament is racially narrowminded. They say the New Testament gives the first indication that God cares for non-Jewish people.

The book of Jonah contradicts that view. It shows, instead, that God wanted to use Jews like Jonah as agents of his concern. They would preach doom but always with the hope that the warning would lead to repentance.

Jonah needed to develop an attitude like God's toward his enemies. Insistently, God led Jonah to this understanding of his own mind and heart. The book of Jonah is a story of a miraculous change in Nineveh, but even more a story of miraculous change in Jonah.

How to Read Jonah

Like Esther and Ruth, Jonah is a delightful short narrative by a master writer. Its spiritual implications are powerful and obvious. You can easily read it at one sitting.

As you read Jonah, notice the changes that the city of Nineveh goes through. Try also to trace the changes that occur in Jonah, and observe how God pushes him to make these changes. Then ask yourself: what did this book say to its original Jewish readers? What does it say to me?

You may also be interested in following Nineveh's entire history. Though the Ninevites repented in Jonah's time, they later returned to old patterns. Later prophets (Nahum and Zephaniah) predicted Nineveh's downfall for "endless cruelty" (Nahum 3:19), and in 612 B.C. that city was destroyed, never to be inhabited again. A Bible dictionary can summarize Nineveh's long history as a world power; look under "Assyria."

Is Jonah a "fish story"? Interpreters differ over whether it should be read as a parable (not necessarily factual) or as historical fact. At least one reliable account exists of a man swallowed by a sperm whale and later found, alive, in the whale's stomach. Jonah's historical basis cannot be dismissed simply because of the "great fish."

More to the point, Jesus compared himself to Jonah, and the people of his time to Nineveh (Matthew 12:39-41; Luke 11:29-32). He predicted that "the men of Nineveh will stand up at the judgment with this generation and condemn it; for they repented at the preaching of Jonah, and now one greater than Jonah is here." It is hard to see how fictional characters could stand up at an event Jesus evidently believed would be historical.

Notes

MICAH

INTRODUCTION

Light in a Dark Time

Evil and violence were creeping south toward Jerusalem

Country boys often lose perspective in the big city. They gawk at the tall buildings, the fancy clothes, and the showy symbols of power. Micah was a country boy from Moresheth, a small village in the no-man's land southwest of Jerusalem. While his contemporary, Isaiah, moved in and out of the king's palace, Micah shows no sign of traveling in such circles.

Yet this country boy kept his sense of perspective. The blood and violence of his day did not overwhelm him, nor was he intimidated by powerful and wealthy people. He spoke like a person who had seen the world through God's eyes.

Micah lived in one of the darkest times in Israel's history, a time of brutal warfare. The country had long been split into North and South. Micah saw war break out between these sides, with 120,000 deaths on the Southern side alone (2 Chronicles 28:6). Then Assyria, the brutal chief power of the day, smashed the Northern Kingdom after a three-year siege of its capital, Samaria. Only a miracle kept those same Assyrian armies out of Jerusalem (2 Chronicles 32). But for how long would the South remain free?

The Sin of the South

Micah had no doubt how to interpret these chaotic events. God had punished the Northern nation of Israel for sins summarized in 2 Kings 17:16-17: idolatry, Baal worship, child sacrifice, magic and sorcery. Now these same activities were creeping south into Judah—so much so that Micah referred in disgust to Jerusalem as a "high place," the traditional setting for pagan idol worship (1:5). The same judgment the North had suffered would come to Judah if people continued to disobey God.

Other historical accounts give more details of the South's sins. They describe how King Ahaz set up a foreign altar in God's temple, altering the temple construction "in deference to the king of Assyria" (2 Kings 16:18). He gave his own children in human sacrifice and shut the Lord's temple, substituting altars on every street corner (2 Chronicles 28:3,24-25). Along with this religious corruption came every other kind of sin: dishonesty (Micah 6:10-11), bribery (3:11), injustice (2:2), and distrust that destroyed families (7:5-6).

Beyond the Darkness

Yet Micah saw light ahead. He perceived a majestic God over all events, who punished his people only to purify and restore them. Along with making some of the Bible's frankest predictions of destruction, Micah gave some of the clearest predictions of the Messiah, the leader who would come to save Israel. Micah's perspective encompassed not only the events of his time but events far in the future, when the nations "will beat their swords into plowshares" (4:3).

Micah looked straight at the darkness of his time and at the darkness yet to come. But his perspective—God's perspective—enabled him to see beyond darkness. "Do not gloat over me, my enemy! Though I have fallen, I will rise. Though I sit in darkness, the Lord will be my light" (7:8).

How to Read Micah

Micah had the big view of history, and thus he covered a lot of ground. His book, only seven chapters, is loaded with pronouncements on the events of several thousand years. Because so much is jammed into so short a space, reading Micah can be confusing. A fragment may deal with the Messiah, for instance, and without warning the next few verses shift to the battle against Assyria.

To grasp Micah's message, think of his book as a collection of short speeches. One speech doesn't necessarily lead into the next. Instead of reading quickly from start to finish, pause after each short section to see whether you understand what it says. Try to understand who is speaking. Sometimes God speaks, sometimes Micah, sometimes the rebellious people.

In general, Micah follows this outline: chapters 1-3 indict both Northern and Southern Kingdoms, with their leaders; chapters 4 and 5 turn to the wonderful future God is planning; the last two chapters give the trial, punishment, and hope of the guilty nations.

It's very helpful to understand Micah's historical situation. Micah 1:1 names the kings of Judah he worked under. You can read about these kings, and their Northern counterparts, in 2 Kings 15:27–20:21 and 2 Chronicles 27–32.

Notes

_____

_____

_____

_____

_____

NAHUM

God's Answer to Injustice

A power above the powers

Is life fair? It rarely seems so, especially in international politics. The most vicious dictators thrive, and raw power is the key ingredient in a successful foreign policy. Weak people get trampled.

As a citizen of Judah, the prophet Nahum felt the force of such injustice. His message from God concerned the greatest city of the time, Nineveh. This city, the capital of Assyria, represented raw, brutal power—"endless cruelty," as Nahum put it (3:19). Though Nineveh was hundreds of miles northeast of Judah, her power dominated the Middle East. In contrast, Judah was a small, fragile state barely clinging to independence.

Nahum's Nerve

Judah's sister nation to the north, Israel, had already been defeated by Assyria and carried into exile. Only God's miraculous intervention had saved Judah on that occasion. And now, in Nahum's time, the Assyrians had returned. They dragged off Manasseh, the king, with a hook in his nose (2 Chronicles 33:11). Judah was forced to pay tribute as a vassal state.

Few people can stare into the face of such raw power and come away unimpressed. Nahum did so only because he had seen a far greater power—the power of a God whose wrath could shatter rocks. If God was angry, how could Nineveh stand? Nahum's absolute confidence in God is underlined throughout this book.

It took nerve to stand up and predict the downfall of the most powerful nation in the world. Yet, in this book, Nahum sounds unintimidated, almost lordly. He spoke with confidence because he knew God's character: "The LORD will not leave the guilty unpunished" (1:3).

Decline and Fall of Nineveh

Within a few years, Nahum's predictions came true. Nineveh did fall, never to rise again. The greatest city in the world became a pile of rubble overgrown with grass. Both Alexander the Great and Napoleon camped near it but had no idea a city had ever been there. The site became known as "the mound of many sheep."

The name *Nahum* means "comfort." Though Nahum describes God's anger, his message offers comfort to those who live with injustice and evil. "The LORD is good," said Nahum, "a refuge in times of trouble. He cares for those who trust in him, but with an overwhelming flood . . . he will pursue his foes into darkness" (1:7-8). Nineveh is gone, but Nahum's testimony lives on, reminding us that though God's justice seems slow, nothing can ultimately escape it.

How to Read Nahum

Nahum stands out from the other short prophetic books in two ways. He addressed a foreign city—Nineveh—instead of his own home nation, and he used unusually vivid language.

You can read more background on Judah and its relationship to Nineveh in the following historical accounts: 2 Kings 17–19 and 2 Chronicles 32–33:13. The background will help you understand why God was so angry at Nineveh.

As you read Nahum, pay special attention to the vivid imagery. Some of the best examples are the following:

Descriptions of warfare: 2:3-7; 3:1-3

Nineveh like a pool with its water draining out: 2:8

Nineveh like a lions' den, full of bones, 2:11-12

Nineveh like a prostitute shamed in the streets: 3:5-6

Nineveh's fortresses like fig trees, with fruit shaken into the mouth of their attacker: 3:12

Nineveh's numerous citizens like grasshoppers: prolific, voracious, and quickly disappearing: 3:15-17

Notes

_____

_____

_____

_____

_____

HABAKKUK

INTRODUCTION

The Problem of Evil

Habakkuk's question: "Why is God silent while the wicked succeed?"

The book of Habakkuk begins with a complaint. The prophet saw injustice, violence, and evil in his own country, yet God remained silent and invisible. Why didn't God intervene? Why did he give no answer when Habakkuk called out for help? Habakkuk took these questions directly to God, in prayer.

God answered him, but hardly in the way Habakkuk had anticipated. God said he was sending the Babylonians to punish Judah. God's words described a ruthless, savage army that would tear Israel apart.

So Habakkuk complained again. Could this be justice—punishing Judah through an even more evil nation? Deeply perplexed, Habakkuk waited to see what answer God would give to his second complaint.

How long he had to wait, we do not know. But God did reply, and his answer is perhaps the best explanation we have of God's attitude toward evil. It satisfied Habakkuk, so that his book, which begins with a complaint, ends with one of the most beautiful songs in the Bible.

Two Certainties to Live By

God pointed out two certainties to Habakkuk. First, the violent, proud Babylonians would be paid back with the very weapons they had used on others. Just as they destroyed nations, they would be destroyed. "Has not the LORD Almighty determined . . . that the nations exhaust themselves for nothing?" (2:13). Evil may dominate the earth, but it always wears itself out.

The second certainty was God's character. He may be silent for a time, but not forever. "The earth will be filled with the knowledge of the glory of the LORD, as the waters cover the sea" (2:14). In chapter 3, Habakkuk "saw" this powerful glory, and his heart pounded. It changed his attitude from complaining to joy.

Because the future belongs to God, a believer can cling to the truth embodied in 2:4: "The righteous shall live by his faith." Habakkuk beautifully expressed this attitude of faith in the last three verses of his book: no matter how hard life might become, he would rejoice and find strength in the Lord.

Living by Faith

Did Habakkuk explain why God allows evil? Not precisely. He did affirm that God has not lost control. Evil is moving toward its own logical end of self-destruction, and God's glory will someday fill the earth. Habakkuk offers no proof of this, merely the record of God's communication to him. A believer can find hope and joy through faith in God, regardless of circumstances. Habakkuk's capsule of faith was quoted at three crucial points in the New Testament: Romans 1:17; Galatians 3:11; and Hebrews 10:38.

Though Habakkuk probably did not live to see it, the Babylonians were destroyed. Today they are merely a memory. Yet we, like Habakkuk, must still wait in faith to see the earth "filled with the knowledge of the glory of the LORD."

How to Read Habakkuk

Other prophets carried messages from God to humankind; Habakkuk addressed God alone. He pondered deep riddles of life while wrestling with two terrible realities: the degeneration of his own nation and the certainty that it was about to be overrun by another, worse nation. How can a just God allow, even use, such evil? To fully delve into Habakkuk's questions, you may want to read the book of Job and Psalm 73, which explore related issues.

The first two chapters of Habakkuk tell of two "complaints" and two answers. As you read, try to imagine the emotional changes Habakkuk experienced as he talked with God. Then read the joyful psalm of chapter 3 (set to music, either by Habakkuk or someone else) and ask yourself: where did this joyful confidence come from?

Notes

ZEPHANIAH

Beyond Darkness

A worldwide catastrophe and a shining light

Zephaniah wrote not long after Manasseh had ended his 50-year reign in Judah. One of the worst kings on record, Manasseh had made idol worship and child sacrifice common practice. He had built altars for star worshipers in God's temple and had encouraged male prostitution as part of the religious ritual. He had also "shed so much innocent blood that he filled Jerusalem from end to end . . . " (2 Kings 21:16). His son Amon carried on in the same way during his short reign.

Then came King Josiah, who took the throne at the age of eight, after his father's assassination. The Bible says there was never a king like Josiah (2 Kings 23:25). He led a reform, destroying all the pagan idols and restoring the temple. He organized the first Passover celebration in generations.

Zephaniah, who was probably related to the king through his great great grandfather King Hezekiah, apparently spoke just before the big changes. The nation's future hung in the balance, and Zephaniah's words may well have helped tip it toward renewal of faith in God.

From Gloom to Exultation

Zephaniah's book begins in deep gloom. Like other prophets, he condemned the sins of his nation and predicted judgment from God. But he went one big step further. He talked repeatedly about "the day of the LORD," and saw that it would be a supernatural event sweeping clean the whole planet. Zephaniah offered no hope that it could be avoided. The Lord had warned and pleaded, but to no avail (3:6-7). Zephaniah saw hope for a minority only. A faithful, humble remnant could be sheltered from disaster if they would seek God.

Beyond the judgment fires Zephaniah saw something remarkably bright. He predicted that a purified remnant of God's people, truthful and humble, would trust in God. He foresaw a remade world learning to worship God.

Therefore this short book, which starts with such gloom, ends with an ecstatic song of joy: an anticipation of the kingdom to come after the judgment. God's blessing will flow freely as every nation worships him. Zephaniah's words may have been influential in encouraging Josiah's reforms, but his vision extended far beyond. The New Testament speaks often, like Zephaniah, of the worldwide judgment and a renewed world to come.

How to Read Zephaniah

Zephaniah will seem more interesting if you grasp the historical situation in which he wrote. For the decadence that led to King Josiah's reforms, read 2 Kings 21. Josiah's history is told in chapters 22 and 23. Second Chronicles 33-35 tells the same story with slightly different details.

Zephaniah is easily understood. It has a clear and symmetrical structure, opening (after a brief introduction) with a warning of judgment for Judah and its capital of Jerusalem, then extending the judgment to Judah's neighbors, and closing in chapter 3 with good news about Jerusalem.

Notes

_____

_____

_____

_____

_____

INTRODUCTION

The Prophet Who Got Results
For once, God's people listened

Sometimes, at crucial moments, a single voice can stir a directionless mass of people to action. Winston Churchill's inspiring oratory may have saved Britain in World War II. Martin Luther King's sermons and speeches captured America's conscience in the 1950s and 60s.

Haggai's words, similarly, rang clear in a time of confusion. The Jews had come back from their exile in Babylon nearly 20 years before. But they seemed to have forgotten the point of returning. After one false start on the temple, the exiles had devoted their energy to building their own houses. The ruins of Solomon's temple stood as a nagging reminder that they had neglected God.

Now Haggai urged these pioneers to "give careful thought" to their situation. He did not rage like Jeremiah or build eloquent poems like Isaiah. He put it simply and logically. They had worked hard, but what had it earned them? Their crops were unsuccessful. Their money disappeared as soon as they earned it. Why? Haggai asked. Because they had mistaken their priorities. They needed to put God first. They needed to rebuild his temple.

A Response from the Heart

People responded to Haggai immediately. Prophets before him, such as Amos, Isaiah, or Jeremiah, had spoken for decades without seeing such a heartfelt reaction. Haggai's messages span a mere four months, but he accomplished everything he set out to do. In four years the temple was complete.

What made the temple so important? After all, the proper sacrifices and rituals could be carried out on a makeshift altar. But God's reputation was at stake. He could not be properly honored so long as the house he called home lay in ruins. The temple symbolized God's presence, and Israel's priorities.

Would rebuilding the temple change Israel's financial situation? Haggai's first words promised nothing. He simply said, "Give careful thought to your ways," and pointed out that Israel's lack of prosperity was God's doing. They had worked hard, but God had withheld the rain their crops needed. A month later (2:1-9) Haggai said that God had glorious plans for Israel, plans that would shake the whole earth. But he referred to God's presence with them, not to good crops.

Only on the last day accounted for in this brief book did Haggai get back to the subject of harvests. He said that God wanted his people to "give careful thought" again—this time to the dramatic difference they would see in their harvests since they had put God first. "From this day on I will bless you," God said through Haggai.

How to Read Haggai

One of the shortest books in the Bible, Haggai can easily be read at a sitting. Haggai's words came at a critical time in the life of the nation of Israel. They mark one of the few times in all history when God spoke and his people quickly and unquestioningly obeyed. For the historical background, read Ezra 1-6. Haggai's crucial message is mentioned in Ezra 5:1-2.

There is a progression to God's warnings and his promises through Haggai. Study each of Haggai's messages, and note down what *encouragement*, what *warning*, and what *hope* God offered Israel. How did God motivate them to obey him?

Notes

_____

_____

_____

_____

_____

ZECHARIAH

INTRODUCTION

Starting Over

How could they rebuild with broken pieces?

When the Jews reviewed their history, it looked like a long slide downhill. Consistently, they had responded to God's love by grumbling against him, by disobeying his law, by worshiping idols. Finally, after centuries of warning, punishment had come. Jerusalem was flattened. The survivors marched off in chains toward the other end of the world.

They had not merely lost a battle. They had lost, seemingly, their place in God's heart and their future as his special people.

But hope for a new start came in exile. When Persian emperor Cyrus took power, he offered Jews a chance to return to their land and rebuild their temple. Some jumped at the chance. They took the long journey to a homeland most of them had never seen (you can read about the trip in the first chapters of Ezra). They wanted not merely to rebuild; they hoped somehow to escape the downward, anti-God trend that had plagued their nation from its beginnings.

Hope Begins to Fade

They found a disheartening scene. Their once-beautiful city was a ghost town. Everything of value had been destroyed. Fertile fields were overgrown. The region was almost empty of people.

The small band of returned exiles built an altar on the grounds of the ruined temple. But soon they grew discouraged about actual rebuilding. They had enough trouble finding shelter and eking out a living from the land. When their non-Jewish neighbors fought against rebuilding the temple, the former exiles gave up. Their hopes of a glorious "new beginning" began to fade.

The temple stayed in a state of disrepair for nearly 20 years, until the prophets Haggai and Zechariah stirred up renewed interest. These prophets saw that as long as the temple lay in ruins, Israel's distinctive character as a people of God was ruined, too. At their urging, the Jews organized to build again.

The book of Zechariah is a record from that critical period of rebuilding. Its first recorded message dates from approximately two months after the temple foundation was laid. The temple was completed four years later, at least partly due to Zechariah's encouraging words.

Needed: A Change of Heart

Zechariah wasn't mainly interested in a building, however. More important was the relationship with God that the temple symbolized. In his first recorded words Zechariah warned his people not to be like their ancestors. What good had a temple done them? A really new beginning required a change of heart. " 'Return to me,' declares the LORD Almighty, 'and I will return to you' " (1:3).

The last half of Zechariah widens its view to the whole world. The small refugee community of Jews, Zechariah says, holds the world's future. Their new beginning would become the hope of the world.

How to Read Zechariah

Most people find Zechariah difficult to understand. Throughout the book you will find references to people and events that are hard to interpret. A commentary can be a great help, clarifying the meaning of these details. For historical background on Zechariah's times, read Ezra 1-6. Zechariah is mentioned by name in Ezra 5:1.

The book of Zechariah breaks into three parts. The first six chapters offer eight symbolic visions, which were meant to encourage the builders of the temple. They are not too difficult to understand if you take them one at a time and don't rush through them. Their main emphasis: God is at work again. He plans to live with his people in Jerusalem. He will protect them from their enemies, cleanse them from their sins, banish evil. He is making a new beginning for them.

Chapters 7-8 address the quality of life God wants his renewed people to enjoy. These words contain many encouraging promises to Israel.

The last six chapters are packed with puzzling references to the struggles Israel must endure in becoming what God wants. You will find predictions of terrible suffering and absolute victory. These chapters, as complex as they are, helped the Gospel writers understand Jesus' suffering, death, and resurrection. The writers quoted these chapters as they wrote of Jesus' final days. The book of Revelation, telling of the final goal of history, also drew on Zechariah's predictions.

Notes

_____

_____

_____

_____

_____

MALACHI

INTRODUCTION

When Faith Grows Weary

Malachi spoke to people "going through the motions"

Success has dangers of its own. When you reach the top, you may tend to slack off. Spiritual life can gradually deteriorate too.

Malachi, in this short book, tried to awaken Israel from slackness in relating to God. Years before, they had optimistically returned to Jerusalem after a long exile. Their faith had grown deeper through difficulties. Despite fierce opposition they had rebuilt the temple, the symbol of their hope in God. They had expected God to supernaturally fill it with his glory and make their nation the center of the world.

By Malachi's time Israel's hope had faded. In fact, life seemed to have passed the Israelites by.

They could not see that God loved them (1:2), and they felt that serving God brought no reward (2:17; 3:14).

No Big Sinners

The people of Jerusalem had become lukewarm. Their complaints showed it, and so did their actions. They were not "big" sinners like the people before the exile, who had practiced child sacrifice and brought idols into the temple. Malachi's people had kept their religion, but they had lost contact with the God whom the religion was all about.

While Malachi mentioned the same injustices and evils earlier prophets had blasted (3:5), he concentrated most of his energy on problems that may seem petty in comparison: mixed marriages, divorce, and apathetic worship (shown in their second-rate offerings). Through

Malachi's eyes, we see the Israelites going through the motions of their faith, doing the bare minimum.

How do you heat up a lukewarm faith? Malachi used several tactics. He began with God's love. To his audience, it was not apparent. But if they would compare their situation with neighboring Edom's, they would see that God had been caring for them all along.

Curing a Careless Attitude

Malachi then challenged the Jews to take obedience seriously. They were bringing injured or sick animals to God for offerings. "Try offering them to your governor!" Malachi said. "Would he be pleased with you?" (1:8). Malachi urged them to bring the perfect animals God's law demands and his honor requires. Malachi further demanded that they stop marrying women of other religions, a practice that inevitably introduced religious compromise. They must also put an end to divorce. And finally, they must bring a full tenth—the "tithe"—of their income to God at the temple. Their skimping amounted to robbery—robbery from God.

Malachi didn't demand these changes just because they were in the rulebook. They were actions meant to symbolize an inner attitude. The people must practice their faith seriously. " 'Test me in this,' says the LORD Almighty, 'and see if I will not throw open the floodgates of heaven and pour out so much blessing that you will not have room enough for it' " (3:10).

The Last Voice

Malachi's was the last Old Testament voice. It reverberated through 400 or more years of biblical silence. During those years at least some of Malachi's message took hold. Led by the Pharisees, Jews became increasingly devoted to keeping the Old Testament law. Unfortunately, many of them lost Malachi's main point. They forgot that the law was not an end in itself. It was a means by which to give God the honor he deserves.

How to Read Malachi

God's voice dominates Malachi, the voice of a loving father pleading with his children. The people's reponse is given in the form of seven questions or complaints. The result is a kind of dialogue—almost an argument—which lets you see into the personal attitudes of God and the people he is speaking to.

As in most arguments, a variety of issues are raised, but they are all rooted in a few basic attitudes. As you read through Malachi, try to see what attitudes lay behind the questions, complaints, and problems of God's people. Also note what attitudes lay behind God's words and promises to them.

Notes

_____

_____

_____

_____

MATTHEW

INTRODUCTION

A Bridge from Old to New

Why start with a list of names?

For four hundred years, nothing new was added to the Bible. The prophets fell silent. During this time, Middle Eastern empires rose and fell, and the tiny nation of Israel suffered under the domination of greater powers like Greece and Rome.

And then, something momentous happened. A baby was born—a baby unlike any who had ever come before. By introducing this baby who grew into the man Jesus, the book of Matthew opens a whole new section of the Bible—the New Testament.

Matthew makes his intentions clear from the very first sentence: he connects Jesus' arrival with the Old Testament story line. Jesus was a Jew, he says, the son of Abraham. And also a king, the son of David. Matthew then sets out to prove an audacious claim: this Jesus, from the humble town of Nazareth, is the very "Messiah," the deliverer promised back in the Old Testament. (*Christ* is a Greek translation of the word *Messiah*).

Jesus' Family Tree

People all over the world, especially Jews, had been eagerly awaiting the Messiah. His coming would change the entire history of the world, they believed. Could this carpenter's son be the long-expected king? To answer that question, Matthew starts with a genealogy.

Genealogies—long lists of names—rarely prove interesting to anyone but the people directly involved. To those people, however, the lists are anything but boring.

Listen to one modern author describe what it was like to hear an ancient genealogy: "There is an expression, 'the peak experience,' a moment which emotionally can never again be equaled in your life. I had mine, that first day in the village of Juffure, in black west Africa . . . Goose bumps came out on me the size of marbles." With those words, Alex Haley, author of *Roots*, recalls the day he first heard, from the lips of an aged storyteller, the account of young Kunta Kinte being taken captive by slave traders in 1752.

The Importance of Roots

Haley's ancestors in Tennessee and Virginia had descended directly from a native African captured in a tiny village in Gambia. The day he listened to the gentle African elder recite, "And so-and-so took as a wife so-and-so, and begat so-and-so," the final link in Haley's family chain snapped into place. *Roots* tells the story of this connection.

In a similar way, the book of Matthew doesn't begin with Jesus' birth, but reaches back further to establish his roots. If indeed Jesus is the Messiah, his ancestors must match up to that claim. As any student of history knows, kings don't merely declare themselves; they must belong to a royal line. Matthew traces Jesus' lineage to the father of the Jewish race, Abraham—who first received the promise of the Messiah—then to the great Jewish king, David.

Links to the Old Testament

After recording Jesus' bloodline, Matthew narrates the story of Jesus' life on earth. He relies heavily on the Old Testament, quoting it more frequently than does any other New Testament author. (Note such phrases as "that it might be fulfilled as was spoken by the prophets.")

The first book in the New Testament, then, stands as the Gospel that pulls things together, the link between the old and the new. Matthew starts with Jesus' roots, but he also contrasts Jesus with the traditional Jewish picture of the Messiah. Jesus, a king, ended thousands of years of eager waiting. But he came to establish a wholly new kind of kingdom—a kingdom different from what anyone expected.

How to Read Matthew

Anybody who has looked over an Internal Revenue Service (IRS) form knows what tax collectors like: neat, orderly rows of figures, with all expenses and income classified by type and source. Fittingly, the Gospel attributed to former tax collector Matthew reflects systematic, ledger-sheet thinking. He doesn't tell Jesus' story chronologically; he groups facts topically.

Matthew collects Jesus' sayings in five main places. First comes the famous Sermon on the Mount in chapters 5-7. Chapter 10 records Jesus' instructions to his disciples' about their mission; chapter 13, a series of parables on the kingdom; chapter 18, Christ's words on the church as a community; and chapters 23-25, Jesus' thoughts on religious hypocrisy and his predictions of the future. Sandwiched in among these five great discourses you'll find connected scenes of Jesus in action.

The skillful blending of Jesus' action and teaching has helped earn this Gospel an esteemed place in literature. Artists are often drawn to it as a capsule summary of Jesus' ministry: witness J.S. Bach's greatest choral work, *St. Matthew's Passion*, the joyous play *Godspell*, and Pasolini's film *The Gospel according to St. Matthew*. The French skeptic Renan praised Matthew as "the most important book of Christendom—the most important book that has ever been written."

Two approaches will help in a detailed study of Matthew. First, consider how it differs from the other three Gospels; this will give you some idea of Matthew's distinctive purpose. Then, you will find it enlightening to look up many of Matthew's references to the Old Testament. Most are cited in footnotes.

Notes

_____

_____

_____

_____

_____

MARK

INTRODUCTION

The Fast-paced Gospel

Mark reads like the script for an action movie

Brief introductory credits flash on the screen. Then the camera pans across an expanse of bleached sand, inhabited mostly by scorpions, lizards, and tarantulas. At last, through the shimmering heat, a lone figure appears: an eccentric wearing camel's hair and crying something in the thin desert air. So begins Mark.

It helps to imagine the book of Mark as a concisely edited documentary film. Unlike the other Gospels, this one has little tolerance for dialogue and personal reflection. The author is writing to a restless, impatient audience—people more like moviegoers than readers.

Mark deftly controls camera angles, alternately panning across large crowds and zooming in on individual people. He leaves no doubt about the main character. After the opening shot of John the Baptist, he moves Jesus to center stage and the camera follows him everywhere.

An Emphasis on Action

Those who look for an outline in Mark come away baffled: all the spliced-together scenes defy structure. One author observed that Mark shows Jesus "scattering miracles like rice at a wedding." Matthew and Luke each give four chapters of historical warm-up before recording a miracle by Jesus; Mark covers three miracles and a group event in the first chapter alone.

In contrast to all its action scenes, the book includes only a sampling of Jesus' parables. It focuses on events, not speeches or editorial comments. Mark shows gymnasium-size crowds pressing around Jesus so tightly that he launches a boat to escape them. Wherever he goes, the crowds follow, buzzing about his remarkable life. "Is he the Holy One of God?" "Is he mad?" "Isn't this the carpenter's boy?"

A Breathless Pace

By dispensing with all but bare-bones action, Mark manages to achieve more drama than perhaps any other biblical writer. Action guarantees an attentive audience, and Mark jams sequences together breathlessly. The heavens open _immediately_; the Spirit sends Jesus into the wilderness _immediately_; he calls his disciples _immediately_—42 times this book uses that hurry-up adverb (in Greek).

Characters rush from place to place, jostle among crowds, are astonished at mighty works. Mark is a Gospel of exclamation points, full of words like _amazed, overwhelmed, terrified_. A phenomenon is loose on the earth, and the author is determined to capture its impact for future generations.

How to Read Mark

About 90% of Mark's content appears in the other three Gospels, but the book makes an ideal starting place for someone who knows little about Jesus. Its style—simple sentences, without complicated transitions or long speeches—makes understanding easier. In fact, Mark was probably written as a missionary book to people who knew next to nothing about the new Christian faith.

Except where he cites Jesus' own quotations, Mark quotes the Old Testament directly in only one place (1:2-3). In addition, Mark doesn't refer to the Old Testament Law, a striking difference from the other Gospels. Such facts indicate his book was written to a non-Jewish audience, probably the Romans.

You'll need no special instructions on reading Mark. This book's breezy style makes it as understandable as a newspaper. Because it loosely follows the chronology of Jesus' life, Mark offers an excellent introduction to the life of Jesus. As you read, stop and ponder the events Mark records. Why did Mark select these facts? What meaning did they have for the people in Jesus day? What about for you?

Notes

_____

_____

_____

_____

_____

LUKE

INTRODUCTION

Like a Joy-filled Musical

Something was brewing on planet Earth

Although Luke covers the same basic territory as Matthew and Mark, he gives away his own slant in the very first chapters. Matthew begins with a formal family genealogy; Mark opens with a bleached-desert scene. In contrast, Luke describes a hearty celebration.

The way Luke tells it, events surrounding Jesus' birth resembled a joy-filled musical. Characters crowded into the scene: a white-haired great uncle, an astonished virgin, a tottery old prophetess. They all smiled broadly and, as likely as not, burst into song.

Once Mary had recovered from the shock of seeing an angel, she let loose with a beautiful hymn. The old priest Zechariah broke nine months of muteness with a rousing poem, and even the unborn John the Baptist kicked for joy inside his mother's womb (1:44). When Jesus finally made an entrance, in an inconspicuous stable, the sky filled with singing angels. Clearly, something was brewing on planet Earth.

History Split in Two

You get the feeling when you read his account that Luke wanted to capture in words the spirit of "great joy" that the angel predicted (2:10). Among dreary, defeated villagers in a remote corner of the Roman Empire, something climactically good was bursting out.

The author tells us (1:1-4) that he researched many accounts of Jesus' life. Intimate details in these first two chapters show he relied heavily on eyewitnesses, for no other Gospel writer picked up so many facts. Careful attention to detail and an undergirding tone of joy characterize Luke's book.

Jesus' birth literally split history into two parts; we memorialize the event whenever we write a date. The book of Luke takes us back to the world before there was an A.D. or B.C., when Jesus' life was just beginning.

Even now, almost 2,000 years later, the commemoration of Jesus' birth still gives cause for joy. We eat better during the Christmas season, buy gifts for others, donate to charity, and sing more often. Our feelings of celebration are gentle aftershocks, reminders of the remarkable moment when God became a man and lived on earth.

How to Read Luke

Luke probably did not know Jesus personally. But as a dedicated convert in the early church, he accompanied the apostle Paul on missionary trips. In three of his letters, Paul refers to Luke with great affection.

As he mentions in his introduction, Luke eventually saw the need to draw up a carefully researched account of the life of Christ. Many accounts of varying quality existed then, but Luke set out to interview eyewitnesses and compose a thoughtful summary. His book shows thoroughness and detail. It starts before Jesus' birth, and ends with his ascension into heaven.

You should find Luke a very appealing book to read. Luke was a gifted writer, and the stories he records have won their place among the classics of literature: the Good Samaritan, the Lost Son, the Rich Man and Lazarus. If Mark is a Gospel of action, Luke is a Gospel of relationships. It contains very good character descriptions.

Look for the many different ethnic, religious, economic, and social groups in Luke. Think of the diverse groups in a country like the United States today. How do you think each of them would respond to Jesus in the flesh?

Note especially two large sections of Luke that present material found nowhere else: chapters 1-2 and chapters 10-19.

Notes

_____

_____

_____

_____

_____

JOHN

INTRODUCTION

God Breaks the Silence

He spoke in the only way we could truly understand

Unless a person communicates to you, in speech or gestures or even facial expressions, you can't get to know him or her. What goes on behind the mask of skin will always remain a mystery.

God, too, was a mystery until he broke his silence. He spoke once, and all creation sprang to life—quasars, oceans, whales, giraffes, orchids, and beetles. He spoke again, says John, and this time the Word took the form of a man, Jesus Christ. John's book tells the story of that Word who became flesh.

Different from Other Gospels

It's clear from the first few paragraphs that John broke sharply from the style of Matthew, Mark, and Luke. The other Gospel writers focused on events, following Jesus through the bustling marketplaces and villages.

Unlike them, John assumed readers knew the basic facts about Jesus. Instead of focusing on facts, he mulled over the profound meaning of what Jesus had said and done. The book of John reads as if it were written under a great, shady tree by an author who had lots of time for reflection.

In his first sentence, John highlights Christ's nature. There are no Christmas scenes here: no stables, shepherds, or wise men. John tells nothing of Jesus' birth and youth. He introduces him as the adult Son of God. After an eloquent prologue, the book shows John the Baptist humbly pointing to Jesus, "the thongs of whose sandals I am not worthy to untie" (1:27).

Jesus Sent with a Mission

John selected vignettes from no more than 20 days in Jesus' life, and arranged them so that they present a Messiah who knows "where I came from and where I am going" (8:14). Jesus was not simply a "man who fell to earth," but God's Son, sent to do the work of the Father. His repeated references to the One "who sent me" give a cadence to the book.

According to John, Christ participated in the original creation act. But later he was sent to earth as the Word, the sum of all that God wanted to say. God spoke in the only way we could truly understand: by becoming one of us.

How to Read John

New Christians often turn to the book of John because it spells out so clearly the basics of the faith. Jesus proves who he is, diagnoses humanity's problems, and bluntly describes what is necessary for conversion. You will likely recognize familiar verses and phrases in this remarkable book (such as Jesus' "I am" sayings).

John selected seven "signs" or miracles (five of which aren't reported elsewhere) and built a story around them. As you read John, note how the author weaves together his story and its meaning.

It's best to read John in units. Don't just read a paragraph or a chapter. Follow the boldface sectional headings and read a complete section, both the action and the commentary on it. John does not primarily relate events; he interprets those events.

Look carefully for the audiences Jesus addresses. Is he talking to his disciples? To his opponents? To the large crowds? He treats each audience differently.

Notes

_____

_____

_____

_____

_____

ACTS

INTRODUCTION

The Linking Book
Imagine a Bible without the book of Acts

The New Testament divides neatly into two nearly equal sections. The first consists of four Gospels that tell about Jesus' life on earth. The second section, beginning with Romans, concerns churches that sprang up after Jesus left. In between stands the book of Acts.

The best way to appreciate Acts is to imagine a Bible without it. You have just read the life of Jesus, underscored by four different authors, and you turn to Romans: "Paul, a servant of Christ Jesus . . . to all in Rome who are loved by God and called to be saints." Rome? How did the story get there from Jerusalem?

Next you'd find two books, also from Paul (who's he?), addressed to "the church of God in Corinth." Another book follows, written to the church in Galatia, then one to Ephesus, and so on with more letters to other exotic locales. Obviously, something is missing. Without Acts, the New Testament leaps from an orderly history of one man, Jesus, to a collection of unexplained personal correspondence.

A Plan Revealed by Jesus

With Acts, everything fits into place. This book gives a transition from the life of Christ to the new church. It introduces Paul, and explains how a minority religion crossed the sea to Rome, the capital of the Empire. A reader of Acts visits key cities sprinkled around the Mediterranean, meets the principal leaders of the new movement, and gets a strong scent of the problems that will occupy Paul's letters.

Luke, a physician, had written the third Gospel as an account of "all that Jesus began to do and to teach" (Acts 1:1). The book of Acts resumes the story, hinting that this history, too, will show Jesus at work, but in a quite different form. "I will build my church," Jesus had promised (Matthew 16:18), and Acts graphically shows how that process began.

Jesus himself had laid out the plot in his last recorded words on earth: "You will be my witnesses in Jerusalem, and in all Judea and Samaria, and to the ends of the earth" (1:8). Acts faithfully follows that outline: the first seven chapters show the church in Jerusalem, the next five focus on Judea and Samaria, and the rest of the book follows the spread of the gospel to the outposts of Roman civilization.

Boisterous Beginnings

The book opens in Jerusalem, during the Pentecost holiday. Over a million pilgrims were milling about the city when suddenly a group of 120 believers came alive. Jesus' followers hit the streets with a bold new style, and 3,000 joined up on the first day alone. Starting with that boisterous scene, Luke spins a historical adventure tale.

Due to Luke's writing skill, Acts reads like a novel, skipping from one exhilarating scene to the next. Wherever the apostles went, action swirled, riots erupted, and a small church took root. In an era when new religions were a dime a dozen, the Christian faith became a worldwide phenomenon. Acts tells how.

How to Read Acts

Acts reads like well-written history. It follows a logical plan, includes fascinating details, and focuses on the most dramatic events. In that sense, it is self-explanatory.

The first twelve chapters concentrate mainly on the apostle Peter. The rest of Acts features Paul, and the book explains how he became accepted as the first and foremost Christian missionary. Paul made three extensive trips in Acts, then a final voyage in chains to Rome.

Acts records the early history of relations between the church and the Roman empire. It also gives important background information on such cities as Corinth, Ephesus, and Philippi—cities Paul later wrote letters to. The material in Acts will help you understand what Paul is writing about in 1 and 2 Corinthians, Ephesians, Philippians, and the other letters.

Acts also summarizes 18 different speeches by Paul, Peter, and a few others. These speeches make a fascinating study in themselves: the apostles were beginning to interpret the facts of Jesus' life in light of their spiritual significance. As you read them, note how the speakers chose their words and content with the audience in mind, and then note audience reaction.

Notes

_____

_____

_____

_____

_____

ROMANS

INTRODUCTION

A Most Demanding Audience

If you were stranded on a deserted island, what book would you want along?

Imagine yourself in a college speech course. Your assignment: a brief speech on "the meaning of life." Over late-night cups of coffee, you outline the Christian faith and what it means to you.

You devote a lot of time to this assignment—after all, this speech may be the only clear expression of faith your classmates will ever hear.

But what if you were asked to write up the speech for your local paper? Instead of a few dozen listeners, you would have thousands of readers. Undoubtedly, you would devote even more time and care to preparation.

Letter to the Center of the World

Let your imagination run even further. How would you react if you were asked to adapt this same speech for a front-page story in the *New York Times*? This newspaper has sophisticated, demanding readers. In writing for them, you would meticulously pore over every word, polishing phrases and making sure your thoughts were complete and well-expressed.

You can see a similar process at work in the apostle Paul's various letters. Some of his letters were, like a college speech, addressed to a small cluster of people he knew by name. Often they consisted of warm, personal words of advice or even fatherly scolding.

But, *Romans*...the very title of this book conjures up images of the powerful empire that ruled the western world. To people of Paul's day, Rome was the center of the world in every way: law, culture, power, and learning. A letter to this sophisticated audience had to be impressive indeed.

In Romans, Paul brilliantly set down the whole scope of Christian doctrine, which, at that time, was still being passed along orally from town to town. Paul wanted to convince those demanding readers that Christ held the answers to all of life's important questions.

One-Volume Summary

Literary types are often asked questions like this: "What one book would you most want along if you were stranded on a deserted island?" (G.K. Chesterton gave a classic reply: *"Thomas's Guide to Practical Shipbuilding"*!) If asked the same question about a single book of the Bible, many Christians would choose Romans. Compact, yet all-encompassing, it summarizes the Christian faith.

Despite its thoroughness, however, Romans does not read like a dry book of theology. Great revivals in church history have been spawned by a study of this book. Augustine, Martin Luther, and John Wesley all trace their spiritual renewals to a reading of Romans. It gives the apostle Paul's final answer to questions about the "meaning of life."

How to Read Romans

Romans is a book to savor, slowly and carefully. Paul is developing an argument, and his logic unfolds thought by thought from the very first chapter. You may recognize many well-known verses in Romans; note these in their context as a part of Paul's overall presentation.

Romans divides into a clear outline. Chapters 1-3 introduce the book and give the need for the good news of the gospel. The end of chapter 3, called the "central theological passage in the Bible," compresses the core message in a brief paragraph. Chapters 4 and 5 expand on that message.

Romans 6-8 discuss the working out of the gospel in a Christian's life. Paul then pauses for three chapters (9-11) to link his argument to the Old Testament history of the Jews. From there, he proceeds to give practical advice on specific problems (12-16).

It will require time and concentration to grasp fully the teachings of Romans; few people would claim to have "mastered" this book. But it has no equal as a concise, reasonable statement of the Christian faith.

Notes

_____

_____

_____

_____

_____

1 CORINTHIANS

INTRODUCTION

The Last Place to Start a Church
Few expected much from crazy Corinth

Every large city has one pocket where prostitutes, strippers, gamblers, and drug dealers hang out. Tourists stroll by to gawk at the sights. In New York, it's Times Square; in San Francisco, the North Beach district; in New Orleans, Bourbon Street; and in Las Vegas, it's virtually anywhere.

In the ancient world, the whole city of Corinth was known for that kind of lifestyle. Romans made the Corinthians the butt of dirty jokes, and playwrights consistently portrayed them as drunken brawlers. The Greek verb "to Corinthianize" meant to live shamelessly and immorally.

A Wide-Open City

Everyone knew what the Corinthians worshiped: money and the kinky things it could buy. Money flowed freely, for Corinth straddled one of the Roman Empire's most vital trade routes. When a ship wrecked nearby, salvage companies housed the hapless sailors at inflated prices while they scrambled to auction off the ship's cargo. The city was a sprawling open-air market, filled with slaves, Orientals, Jews, Greeks, Egyptians, sailors, athletes, gamblers, and charioteers.

Yet Corinth was no blue-collar town. It had a population of 700,000, second only to Rome's, and as the capital of a large province, the city hosted a parade of Roman diplomats and dignitaries. Its clever citizens showcased new "Corinthian" architecture and prided themselves on having a cosmopolitan outlook.

For their religious ideal, the fun-loving Corinthians adopted Venus, the goddess of love. A temple built in her honor employed more than 1,000 prostitutes.

Paul Takes on the Corinthians

Due to all these influences, Corinth loomed as the one city "least likely to convert" to the Christian faith. What crazy cults and new religions did spring up there quickly gave in to the prevailing good-time atmosphere.

The mighty Paul, reeling from one of his most difficult missionary assignments in Athens, came to Corinth "in weakness and fear, and with much trembling" (2:3). He knew its strategic importance: if the gospel could take root there, it could transplant anywhere—and probably would, considering Corinth's crossroads location.

Paul worked in Corinth for 18 months. To everyone's surprise, the church he founded became one of the largest in the first century. But several years later he heard reports that the church, true to its city's heritage, had broken out in a series of spiritual ills. The distressing news prompted the letter known as 1 Corinthians.

The tone of this letter differs drastically from the one that precedes it. If Romans was stylistically carved in stone, 1 Corinthians was dashed off in tears and anger. One of Paul's longest letters, it covers the greatest variety of topics, partly because the Corinthians added bizarre new twists to ethical issues. In it, Paul gives practical advice on a series of church problems as well as a fascinating glimpse into the personal lives of early Christians.

How to Read 1 Corinthians

To fully appreciate Paul's letters, keep in mind that they are personal correspondence. We are actually reading someone else's mail.

In 1 Corinthians a riled-up apostle gives direct, forthright advice to a troubled local church. Paul saw alarming trends at work, and he used his full literary powers to set its members on the right course. He tried sarcasm, emotional pleas, autobiography, poetry, and lengthy arguments.

First, you will encounter the problems that had been reported to Paul: divisions in the church, a case of incest, court cases, the abuse of Christian freedom, chaos in the worship services. Paul lunges into these problems early in the book. Then, beginning with chapter 7, he takes up some other problems the Corinthians had written him about: marriage and the single life, pagan festivals, behavior of women, spiritual gifts, and the resurrection of the dead.

This first letter to the Corinthians presents a foundation for practical Christian ethics. Use the boldface subtitles throughout the book to locate those issues that especially trouble you. Not all the problems discussed will apply directly to modern situations. But the general principles underlying Paul's advice do apply. As you read, look for those principles behind Paul's arguments.

Notes

_____

_____

_____

_____

_____

2 CORINTHIANS

A Book of Joy and Sadness
Why isn't Paul celebrating his victory?

Athletes sometimes have a strange reaction to a great victory. Some call it "morning-after sickness." An Olympic gymnast who has trained for 15 years wakes up the day after her gold medal performance feeling oddly depressed. Paradoxically, the sweet taste of victory can take on a bitter edge.

An even more pungent feeling may hit those who prevail in personal disputes. The man who wins a crucial court case is stabbed by sympathy for those he defeated. The politician who waves jubilantly to a cheering crowd on primary night winces inwardly at the bruises she suffered—and inflicted—during the campaign. The husband who insisted on a divorce leaves the final settlement feeling sad and burdened.

Lingering Pain

Something like that bittersweet state must have plagued the apostle Paul when he wrote 2 Corinthians. He had just won a great victory in convincing the Corinthians to come over to his side. His spirit had surged upon Titus's news of their wave of support for him (7:6-16). His previous letter, a personal risk, had paid off. Reflecting Paul's triumph, this letter spontaneously breaks out in jubilant praise and thanksgiving.

And yet, in no other letter does Paul so openly admit his frustrations. Immediately after a spare greeting he mentions hardships so severe that "we despaired even of life" (1:8). Numerous references crop up regarding the tense relations he and the Corinthians have had. Paul wonders aloud if he has been too hard on them; he acknowledges his own lingering pain.

A Diary for Two Audiences

Second Corinthians, full of allusions and personal references, reads more like a diary than a public document. If 1 Corinthians analyzes the problems of the Corinthian church, this sequel reveals the problems Paul himself experienced.

He doesn't gloat over his victory in getting the Corinthians' support. Rather, he makes himself vulnerable and opens a window into his inner self. He summarizes his state as "hard pressed on every side, but not crushed; perplexed, but not in despair; persecuted, but not abandoned; struck down, but not destroyed" (4:8-9).

Although random selections from 2 Corinthians demonstrate the author's seesawing moods, the book as a whole reveals a tenacious man on the rebound. Paul expresses relief that the Corinthians' problems are being resolved, even as he points out new danger signs in the church. Always he keeps in mind a dual readership: the majority who support him, for whom he has warm, loving words, and the minority of dissenters who pose a grave threat to church unity.

How to Read 2 Corinthians

Of all Paul's letters, 2 Corinthians reads most like a personal letter and least like a public document. He wrote it when an intense struggle with the Corinthian church was coming to a head. As a result, it reveals much about Paul's troubled state. He half-apologized for speaking so freely, for appearing to be boasting, and for spending time on "foolishness."

Read 2 Corinthians like you would read any personal letter. Try to visualize the mood of the apostle Paul as he was writing, and look between the lines for clues that would help explain his relationship with the church at Corinth. What were his enemies accusing him of? Watch especially for Paul's spirited reply to criticism, especially in the last four chapters. He tells about certain events in his life that are recorded nowhere else.

You will likely notice that Paul is tying up loose ends in this letter: for example, he is preparing for a third visit to Corinth and asking them to get a collection ready. Yet amid these practical matters he pauses to write profound words on such topics as suffering, giving, and personal ministry.

Notes

GALATIANS

INTRODUCTION

No Second-Class Christians

A protest against treason

Paul is angry. You can almost see his face: flushed red, with lines of tension working in his jaw. Typically, he greets his readers briefly and then launches into warm praise of them. But in this letter shock and dismay replace the usual warmth. A crisis threatens the Galatians, and Paul opens with a withering blast against the people responsible.

What's the Problem?

Yet, when you read a few chapters, you may wonder why the apostle is so upset. Galatia seems innocent of the kinkiness of Corinth; Paul describes no incest or idolatry here. Instead, he brings up common, everyday Jewish affairs such as the observance of festival days and the practice of ancient traditions, especially circumcision. Where is the big crisis?

Paul could foresee the outcome of the Galatians' thinking: by unduly stressing their Jewish heritage, the Galatians would soon devalue what Christ had done. They would start trusting in their own human effort (their keeping of "the law") to gain acceptance by God (3:1-5).

If the Galatians continued their policies, the bedrock of the gospel would crumble. Faith in Christ would become just one of many steps in salvation, not the only one. The gospel itself would be perverted (1:6-9).

A Dangerous Class Structure

Paul saw other ominous dangers ahead for the fledgling Christian church. As a Jewish Roman citizen who spoke Greek, he knew well the innate human tendency to look down on people.

Roman citizens snubbed non-Romans; Greeks looked down their noses at Romans; and Jews, with their exalted history and highly developed religion, felt superior to other cultures.

The Galatians' insistence on strict Jewish rules would bring side effects. Subtle distinctions between Christians would inevitably creep in: *faith in Christ is fine, but a circumcised person who keeps the Jewish law...that's far better.* Already, such thoughts had infected two esteemed apostles, Peter and Barnabas. Circumcised Christians were snubbing uncircumcised ones as second-class citizens.

The letter to the Galatians, then, is protesting against treason. It lashes out against subtle dangers that can ultimately pervert the gospel and divide the church. Paul insists that Jesus Christ came to tear down walls between people, not to build them up. In him there is neither Jew nor Greek, slave nor free, male nor female (3:28). Faith in him, not anyone's set of laws (2:16), opens the door to acceptance by God.

How to Read Galatians

Galatians reads like a dramatic court trial. On one side of the courtroom stand Paul's accusers. Persuasive and powerful, these "Judaizers" have followed Paul from town to town, spreading rumors and contradicting his version of the Christian faith.

On the other side sit the jury, the Galatian Christians. They have enjoyed warm friendship with Paul in the past, but some of the charges against him are serious. Did he invent parts of the gospel he preached to them? Has God really given him a special insight? Is it true that his message of "freedom" will lead to a weak, immoral church? Should they turn their backs on their Jewish heritage?

Paul, acting in his own self-defense, paces the courtroom. He uses a variety of debating styles: tight logic, historical reviews, and personal outrage. His integrity, and ultimately Jesus Christ's integrity, is at stake.

In topical content, Galatians covers much the same ground as Romans. But in style, it crackles with a fighting spirit. As you read it, try to visualize that courtroom scene, and judge for yourself Paul's effectiveness as a defendant.

Notes

EPHESIANS

INTRODUCTION

For the Discouraged

Good news for those who feel abandoned and unloved

Imagine yourself a child, abandoned on the streets of New York. Your immigrant parents died on the ship on the way to America. You have no money and no relatives. You can't speak English. And you are left to fend for yourself.

As many as 30,000 orphans found themselves in exactly that predicament in 1850. They slept in alleys, huddling for warmth in boxes or metal drums. To survive, the boys mostly stole, caught rats to eat, or rummaged in garbage cans. Girls sometimes worked as "panel thieves" for prostitutes, slipping their tiny hands through camouflaged openings in the walls to lift a watch or wallet from a preoccupied customer.

Immigrants were flooding New York City then, and no one had the time or money to look after the orphans—no one, that is, except Charles Loring Brace, a 26-year-old minister. Horrified by their plight, he organized a unique solution, the Orphan Train. The idea was simple: pack hundreds of orphans on a train heading west and announce to towns along the way that anyone could claim a new son or daughter when the Orphan Train chugged through.

Adopted into a New Life

By the time the last Orphan Train steamed west in 1929, 100,000 children had found new homes and new lives. Two orphans from such trains became governors, one served as a U.S. congressman, and still another was a U.S. Supreme Court justice.

The Orphan Train provides a vivid parable of the message of Ephesians. To capture Paul's enthusiasm in this book, imagine one more stage in your life as a street urchin in New York.

You have learned to survive and fight off starvation. But one day, someone takes you and puts you on a smoke-belching train jammed with hundreds of other foreign-speaking youngsters. Three days later you are selected by a kindly middle-aged couple in Michigan who introduce themselves as Mr. and Mrs. Henry Ford. You are driven (in an automobile!) to the largest house you have ever seen, and they quietly explain that you are now part of their family. Everything they have is yours to use and enjoy. At long last, by some miracle, you have a family and a home—and what a home!

Welcome to the Family

Paul conveys a feeling something like that in Ephesians, a rich book that expands the message in Jesus' parable of the Lost Son (Luke 15). A big "Welcome Home!" banner is stretched across the lawn, confetti swirls in the air, balloons lunge skyward, and a band plays. Christians have been adopted directly into the family of God. This is a good news book, to put it mildly.

If you feel discouraged or wonder if God really cares or question whether the Christian life is worth the effort, read Ephesians. You will no longer feel like an orphan. Paul describes the "riches in Christ" available to all and points to us, God's adopted children, as his sparkling "Exhibit A" in all the universe (3:10).

Ephesians contains staggering thoughts. Paul wants his readers to grasp "how wide and long and high and deep is the love of Christ" (3:18). He cranks up the volume to express that love, and not one low, mournful note sneaks in.

How to Read Ephesians

In many ways, Ephesians is Paul's "summing-up" book. The same subjects appear in greater detail in books like Romans, 1 Corinthians, and 1 Thessalonians. But in Ephesians, Paul gives an overall view of the grand scheme of the gospel. Only now, Paul says, has God's hidden plan for all of history come to light.

Because it compresses such large thoughts into such a short space, Ephesians deserves very careful study. Read the first three chapters slowly, digesting one paragraph at a time. Such study will prove rewarding: Ephesians gives exuberant good news about the nature of the universe and God's plan for believers.

Like other letters from Paul, Ephesians divides fairly neatly between doctrine (chapters 1-3) and practical advice (4-6). The last half details how our lives should change as a result of the great things described in the first part.

Notes

_____

_____

_____

_____

_____

PHILIPPIANS

INTRODUCTION

Cheerful Sounds from a Jail Cell

Joy when it's least expected

Joy. The word has a quick, poignant ring to it. Yet it, like other words, has been drained of meaning over the years, even tapped as a name for a dishwashing detergent. Nowadays *joy* is used most commonly for a sensation like *thrill*.

We think of joy as something you save up for months to experience and then splurge on in a moment of exhilaration: a trip to Disney World, a free-fall dive, a heart-stopping ride on the world's meanest roller coaster, a hot-air balloon trip. Paul had a different understanding of the word, as this letter reveals.

When You Feel Like Despairing

Philippians uses the word *joy* or *rejoice* every few paragraphs, but the joy it describes doesn't vanish after your heart starts beating normally again. Rejoice, says Paul, when someone selfishly tries to steal the limelight from you. And when you meet persecution for your faith. And when you are facing death.

In fact, the most joyous book in the Bible comes from the pen of an author chained to a Roman guard. Many scholars believe Paul wrote Philippians in Rome just about the time Nero began tossing Christians to ravenous lions and burning them as torches to illuminate his banquets. How could a rational man devote a letter to the topic of joy while his survival was in serious jeopardy? In such an environment, how could joy possibly thrive?

Turning Evil into Good

Paul hints at an answer in a burst of eloquence in chapter 2 (verses 5-11). This pithy, metrical paragraph may have been a hymn familiar to the early church. In it, Paul discusses Christ's perspective in coming to earth.

During the Christmas season we celebrate the grand night God visited earth as a baby. But to the rest of the universe the event looked like an astounding humiliation. God, the Creator of all, took on the unimpressive body of a human being to endure a confining life and grisly death on planet Earth.

Paul points to this death to show that God can take even the darkest moment in history and turn it into good. The cross, and Jesus' not staying dead, proves that nothing is powerful enough to stamp out a reason for joy—joy "in the Lord," as Paul says.

Victory in Jail

Thus even the normally depressing state of imprisonment didn't bother Paul. As he wrote Philippians, he must have recalled his first visit to Philippi. Then, a most unusual jailbreak occurred: the jail broke, but the prisoners didn't (Acts 16:22-28).

Even when Paul stayed in jail for long periods, God used the experience to advance the gospel. As he wrote Philippians, conversions were occurring among the Roman palace soldiers, forced by guard duty to overhear Paul's daily ministry.

Paul summarized his life philosophy in a famous "to be or not to be" soliloquy, concluding that "to live is Christ and to die is gain" (1:21). God is even stronger than death, and that makes a Christian's joy indestructible.

How to Read Philippians

Philippians is simple and straightforward. It's not a formal treatise, but a warm letter to friends. Read it like you would read any personal letter. From the clues Paul gives, try to imagine the relationship between him and the Philippians. What did he like about them? Why were they so important to him?

The Introduction refers to the common use of the words *joy* and *rejoice*. Check out each of these, noticing how Paul can find joy in any circumstances. Use Philippians like a devotional book, first reflecting on what it says, then applying it to your own life.

Notes

_____

_____

_____

_____

_____

COLOSSIANS
INTRODUCTION

Battling the Cults
For everything worthwhile, there exists a counterfeit

You see them in strange outfits on street corners, chanting phrases with too many vowels and punctuating the chants with a noisy tambourine. Or in airports, thrusting books or flowers into your face. Or in California, all over California. You think of them as crazy cults, populated by misfits. Then one day you hear about a friend of yours.

She seemed normal until suddenly, without warning, she snapped. Her parents searched desperately, even hiring private detectives to help get her back. They found her surrounded by allies, with a new name, a new hairstyle, and, so it seemed, a new brain. She stared at them with clear eyes and told them they were missing out on the most wonderful experience of life. She had joined a cult.

A Breeding Ground

Cults come in all varieties, often with exotic names like Hare Krishna or Urantia or the Church of Scientology. They demand much from their members: a lifetime of discipline and absolute loyalty. And they also promise much in return: the pathway to a secret, hidden knowledge available only to those who follow them.

The first-century town of Colosse was a perfect breeding ground for cults. Situated on a major trade route from the East, Colosse entertained a steady stream of Oriental traders with mysterious religious ideas. Even Jews in that area worshiped angels and river spirits.

Early Christian converts soon confronted new variations of the gospel. Then, as now, many cults didn't reject Jesus Christ outright; they merely worked him into a more elaborate scheme. Christ and simple forms of worship, they taught, were fine for beginners, but for the "deep things of God," well, some further steps would be required.

The Best Defense

Paul doesn't give a complete glossary of the "hollow and deceptive philosophy" the Colossians were sorting through. From his arguments, we can gather that the philosophy must have included strains of Jewish legalism mixed in with angel worship, Greek philosophy, and strict self-denial.

The best defense is a good offense. Rather than attacking each peculiar belief point by point, Paul countered with a positive theology. The principles he outlines in this book can be used today to judge new cults.

"Christ is enough," Paul declares. He is God, the fullness of God, the one who made the world, the reason that everything exists. All the mystery and treasure and wisdom you could ask for are found in the person of Jesus Christ; there is no need to look elsewhere.

Approach God Directly

Because Jesus bridged the chasm between God and us, we don't have to approach God indirectly, through a ladder of angels or other gods. We have no need to prove our worth through superior behavior. We can come to God directly and boldly because of Christ.

As for Jewish practices, they were mere shadows, made obsolete by Christ's coming. Why not concentrate on the actual image that God sent to earth?

Before Christ, Paul grants, a mystery was kept hidden for many centuries (1:26). But with Christ, everything broke out into the open. The fullness of God lived, died, and came back from death in broad daylight. Why settle for counterfeits?

How to Read Colossians

Although this letter was written to counter specific problems in the church at Colosse, it includes some of Paul's most eloquent writing about Jesus Christ. Chapter 1 contains a soaring paragraph (1:15-20) that may have been used as a hymn by the early church. Note in this book how Paul concludes all his arguments by referring to Christ.

Chapters 2 and 3 deal with dangerous tendencies in Colosse. Paul argues against a "mystery" religion by firmly asserting Christ is the complete expression of the mystery of God. As you read these two chapters, try to imagine what kind of behavior at Colosse troubled Paul.

Notes

_____

_____

_____

_____

_____

1 THESSALONIANS

What Made Paul Successful?

The apostle fusses over the city that once chased him away

A modern-day evangelist lamented, "Whenever the apostle Paul visited a city, the residents started a riot; when I visit one, they serve tea." The church in Thessalonica, like many of Paul's churches, was born amid violent upheaval. An angry mob took offense at Paul's work and chased him out of town, accusing him of causing "trouble all over the world" (Acts 17:6).

Generally, people do not start riots without a good reason, and in Paul's case they had one. Almost everywhere he visited, an enthusiastic church came to life, provoking the jealousy of the Jewish and Roman establishments.

A Concerned Parent

This letter, 1 Thessalonians, gives important clues into what made Paul so effective at founding churches. Accepted as one of the earliest of Paul's letters, it probably dates from A.D. 50 or 51 and provides a firsthand account of Paul's relationship with a missionary church barely 20 years after Jesus' departure.

Someone once asked John and Charles Wesley's mother which of her ten surviving children she loved the most. She replied, "The one who is sick until he's well, and the one who's away from home until he's back." If someone had asked Paul which church concerned him most, he probably would have answered, "The one with the most problems until it's healthy, the one I've been separated from longest until I return."

When Paul lived with the Thessalonians, he was gentle and loving, "like a mother caring for her little children" (2:7). Later, absent from them, he wrote as if he had only them on his mind all day. In 1 Thessalonians, he praised their strengths, fussed over reports of their weaknesses, and continually thanked God for their spiritual progress.

Questioning Paul's Motives

Some people in the church had questioned Paul's motives, so he opened the letter with a careful review of his work among them. In those days freelance teachers of religion and philosophy sought a profit; Paul reminded the Thessalonians that he had worked night and day to avoid becoming a financial burden. He also painstakingly explained his unavoidable absence from them.

First Thessalonians stands out from the four books that precede it because, unlike them, this letter doesn't major in theology. Rather, it reveals the gratitude, disappointment, and joy of a beloved missionary who can't stop thinking about the church he left behind. Surely one reason for Paul's success centers on his churches' having made as big an impression on Paul as he made on them.

How to Read 1 Thessalonians

This book provides a touching glimpse of Paul as a pastor. Paul visited Thessalonica at a troubled time in his ministry, while enemies were tailing him from town to town (see Acts 16-17). After he left, the church continued to meet hostility.

First Thessalonians is our earliest record of the life of a Christian community. Paul wrote this letter after receiving a mostly positive report (from Timothy) on the Thessalonians' spiritual health. He rejoiced at the good news, but also showed concern over the church's problems.

As you read 1 Thessalonians, notice the issues that Paul addresses: Christians were raising questions about Jesus' return to earth and were disagreeing on matters of morality. But mainly, look for signs of Paul's relationship to the church at Thessalonica.

Notes

_____

_____

_____

_____

_____

2 THESSALONIANS

INTRODUCTION

A Patient Who Didn't Follow Orders

When good advice goes ignored

His light humor and casual manner are gone now. When he was setting the bone, the doctor joked about the benefits of your wearing your arm in a sling every day: instant sympathy from your friends, an opportunity for wild stories on how you got hurt, an easy alibi to avoid heavy work.

But now, three weeks later, lines of concern crease his forehead as he studies the X-rays and notes the slow progress of healing. "I told you to take it easy! Are you giving that arm any rest at all? You can't expect new bone to grow overnight, you know."

When you describe the throbbing pain of the last few days, he grimaces, shakes his head, and scribbles something on a prescription pad. "You shouldn't be feeling pain at this stage," he grumbles. "If you had followed my advice from the beginning you wouldn't need these pills." He then repeats all the instructions he gave you on the first visit, using stronger, less friendly words.

Same Advice, Sterner Words

The book of 2 Thessalonians resembles such a follow-up visit to a family doctor. If you list the topics Paul covers, you will find an uncanny similarity to the subjects of his first letter: Jesus' second coming, spiritual growth, idleness among certain non-workers. However, a sterner, more formal approach replaces the warm tenderness of the first letter.

Obviously, the Thessalonians failed to listen well the first time. Paul wrote this second letter just a few months later, summarizing his message this way: "So then, brothers, stand firm and hold to the teachings we passed on to you, whether by word of mouth or by letter" (2:15). Instead of coaxing, Paul now commands.

Squelching a Rumor

One topic, Jesus' return, dominates 2 Thessalonians more than any other. Church members were stirred up by a false report, allegedly from Paul, claiming the last days had already arrived (2:2). Paul denies the report and outlines several events that must occur before the day of the Lord arrives.

Here, as elsewhere, the Bible does not focus on the last days in an abstract, theoretical way. Rather, it draws a practical application to how we should live. Paul cautions his readers to be patient and steady. He asks them to trust that Jesus' return will finally bring justice to the earth, urges them to live worthily for that day, and commands them not to tolerate idleness—a prescription for health that has equal potency today.

How to Read 2 Thessalonians

Second Thessalonians has many parallels to its companion letter. The Christians in Thessalonica were still struggling with major problems, and each of the three chapters of this book concerns one of them.

Chapter 1 gives encouragement to Christians who were undergoing persecution for their faith. Chapter 2 attacks head-on the false teaching about the day of the Lord. Rumors about the day of the Lord had caused great excitement and speculation, leading to the practical errors Paul addresses in chapter 3.

Paul's specific words about what must happen before the day of the Lord make this letter a key part of New Testament prophecy. The prophecy passages aren't self-explanatory, and may require a Bible reference book for understanding.

Although 2 Thessalonians is Paul's shortest letter to a church, it contains four of his prayers. Note especially his concern for the Thessalonians as expressed in the prayers.

Notes

---

1 TIMOTHY

INTRODUCTION

The Hardest Job

Timothy steps into a hornet's nest

Who has the most difficult job? A brain surgeon? A trapeze artist who risks death with every leap? A nuclear engineer? Or perhaps an air traffic controller, who determines the safety of thousands of passengers. A number of professions might be nominated as the most difficult of all.

But if the apostle Paul were alive today, to that question he would very likely reply, "Without doubt—a pastor's job is hardest." In contrast to professionals who specialize, a pastor must call upon wide-ranging skills. In a given week a pastor may act as a psychologist, priest, social worker, hospital chaplain, administrator, personnel supervisor, philosopher, and communicator.

Paul was acutely aware of the vital nature of such a job. Churches sprouted up wherever he visited, but whether they survived or failed depended largely on what kind of local leadership developed.

Final Words to a Young Friend

To assure that his work would continue, Paul turned more and more to a few loyal friends, especially Timothy and Titus. He wrote them explicit instructions in the three letters that follow, known collectively as "The Pastoral Letters."

Paul wrote 1 Timothy near the end of his life. Rugged years of ministry had passed, years marked by stonings, beatings, jailings, and riots. Paul knew that his age, his enemies, or the increasingly brutal Roman Empire would soon catch up with him.

Timothy, a young man, ranked high in Paul's esteem. Converted during Paul's first missionary journey, he had over the years gained the apostle's complete trust. When a volcano of discontent rumbled in some distant church like Corinth or Thessalonica, Paul quickly dispatched Timothy to try and prevent an eruption.

"I have no one else like him," Paul once wrote of Timothy. "As a son with his father he has served with me in the work of the gospel" (Philippians 2:19,22). Through a swarm of controversies, into prison, on the road—wherever Paul went—Timothy loyally followed. Five of Paul's letters begin with the news that Timothy is at his side.

Timothy Becomes a Pastor

Timothy took on, at Paul's request, that difficult job of heading a local church. The congregation at Ephesus, loose and informal, needed order and a more defined structure. To muddle the scene further, certain members of the church had embraced false doctrines. In this letter, Paul advises his understudy on such matters as worship procedures, the control of unruly women, leadership standards, and policies regarding widows, slaves, and rich people.

Although this book addresses a historical situation from the first century, many problems in the early church—underpaid staff members, a generation gap, an integrity shortage, abuse of social aid, love of money—persist today. A pastor's job description hasn't changed much, or grown any easier, over the centuries.

How to Read 1 Timothy

Despite a weak stomach and timid disposition, Timothy had proved his mettle to Paul in many ways, and Paul wrote this letter to challenge him to a difficult task.

Paul doesn't give many details on the false doctrines Timothy had to combat. These letters, however, include vague hints about super-spiritual living, Jewish genealogies, myths, and fables. Look for the problems Paul alludes to and ask yourself whether they have any modern equivalents.

In his instructions, Paul counseled Timothy to combat heresy not by being forceful and argumentative, but by living an exemplary life and by bringing order to the church. Paul's challenge to live a model life applies directly to us; it remains a powerful prescription for the Christian life.

Notes

_____

_____

_____

_____

_____

2 TIMOTHY

INTRODUCTION

Passing the Torch

The apostle Paul's last known words

Every four years the world watches an ancient ritual unfold: the passing of the Olympic torch. The spectacular pageantry of the opening ceremonies cannot begin until the final carrier of the torch arrives in the stadium. The torch symbolically links the modern Olympic Games to their 2700-year history.

"Passing the torch" has become a familiar phrase, used when the president of General Motors introduces his successor to the public, or when an esteemed orchestra conductor hands over his baton, or a great sports figure tutors her replacement. Often the retiring person delivers an emotional farewell speech. He or she has finished the work; time has come to pass the torch to another.

Choosing Timothy

As the weary apostle Paul neared certain death, with imprisonment preventing him from traveling, he, too, began to think of a successor. It was time to pass the torch, and he decided on the young man Timothy.

At first glance, shy Timothy hardly seemed an adequate replacement, but Paul had few options. "Everyone in the province of Asia has deserted me," he lamented (1:15). This letter, 2 Timothy, reveals his deep reliance on Timothy's loyal friendship. Life was closing in on the apostle, and he felt a somber sense of abandonment.

At times in this letter, Paul lectures Timothy like a master sergeant, calling on him to stand firm, overcome shame, and hold to the faith. Elsewhere, his tone softens into the fond affirmation of a grateful father. Throughout, the bonds of deep friendship are evident: from Paul recalling Timothy's family heritage (1:5) to his urging Timothy to bring him a heavy coat before winter (4:13,21).

An Emotional Moment

Paul's moods alternate between sadness and confidence, nostalgia and grave concern. As he wrote this letter, he contemplated the disquieting months ahead and the prospect of young, divided churches left without his guidance. In these, his last known written words, he sought to prepare Timothy for the inevitable day when the message of God would depend on him and other reliable workers (2:2).

Despite his circumstances, Paul's farewell message from behind bars is gracious, even triumphant. The spreading of the gospel is far too big a task to be limited to any one man. "I am . . . chained like a criminal," Paul declares, "but God's word is not chained" (2:9).

How to Read 2 Timothy

Second Timothy has proved encouraging to Christian workers throughout history. Paul, facing death, did not wallow in self-pity, but instead used this last communication to inspire and challenge his associate Timothy.

This letter reveals much about Paul's emotional state and physical circumstances. As you read it, look for glimpses into Paul's loneliness and suffering. The apostle tells where he turned for strength when he faced personal trials.

In addition, 2 Timothy gives much valuable counsel to those of us who, like Timothy, have inherited the task of representing Christ on earth. Paul stresses the importance of relying on Scripture and of living a life of discipline. As you read this letter, put yourself in Timothy's place; imagine receiving one last personal letter from your great mentor. What final words of advice does he give?

Notes

_____

_____

_____

_____

_____

TITUS

Diverse People, Diverse Problems
An island of liars, brutes, and gluttons

Modern people reading about the past can blur people together into a uniform, faceless crowd of strangers. It's hard to visualize individual people you read about.

Actually, the people Paul addressed were as diverse as those you might meet on the streets of Los Angeles today. Consider Crete, an island populated by five fiercely independent ethnic groups. Its main knowledge of the outside world came through pirates and coarse sailors. Add to that mix a large community of straight-laced Jews, and you can see why the Cretan church was born amid conflict.

Titus the Troubleshooter

When problems erupted in this stormy congregation, Paul dispatched Titus, his trusted associate of 15 years. The book of Galatians (2:1-5) introduced Titus as proof that a non-Jew could become a fully acceptable Christian.

When Titus's name occurs in the New Testament, he is usually seen serving as Paul's troubleshooter, the one called on to deal with local crises. Twice he was sent on a diplomatic mission to the rowdy church at Corinth. This letter indicates he faced an equally challenging task on Crete. Paul wrote the book of Titus as a set of personal instructions on how to handle a difficult assignment.

Because he was writing to people who knew the local circumstances well, Paul rarely bothered to give background for us years-later "over-the-shoulder" readers. But we can gain insights into the conditions by reading between the lines. For example, when Paul tells Titus to search for a leader "not quick-tempered, not given to drunkenness, not violent, not pursuing dishonest gain" (1:7), that description implies something about the average Cretan. One of the island's own poets described Cretans as "always liars, evil brutes, lazy gluttons" (1:12), and the Greeks had even coined a special verb for lying: "to Cretize."

Practical Theology

Titus 2 lists some of the diverse groups in the church: older men, older women, younger women, young men, slaves. Each presented a set of problems that needed attention, and Paul gave Titus specific counsel on each group. Although he was mainly emphasizing the need for good living, Paul also dropped in a few concise restatements of the gospel message. His theology was never distantly theoretical; he applied it to real-life human problems.

Taken as a group, the three pastoral letters (1 and 2 Timothy plus Titus) show Paul, an old man now, learning to rely more and more on capable assistants to carry on his work. The Cretans needed a hard-hitting, practical reminder of "sound doctrine" based on a God "who does not lie" (1:2). The instructions in Titus give the man for whom the book was named—and us—the needed jolt.

How to Read Titus

Like 1 and 2 Timothy, Titus was written to an individual, not a church. This letter has similarities to 1 Timothy, but is less personal and more official. The book of Acts doesn't mention Titus, but 13 references to him in Paul's letters indicate that he was one of Paul's most trusted helpers.

In some letters, such as Galatians, Paul fought valiantly against legalism. But the church on Crete, full of immature Christians, needed basic lessons in morality, and Paul spelled them out for Titus. Using a very straightforward style, he told his associate what he would prescribe in such circumstances.

Because it is written in such a direct style—almost like a training manual—Titus needs little explanation. Paul's meaning comes through clearly. Note particularly how Paul adapts his overall principles to specific groups in chapter 2. And give careful study to the "nuggets" of theology in these passages: 1:1-4, 2:11-14, and 3:4-7.

Notes

_____

_____

_____

_____

_____

PHILEMON

Letter to a Slave Owner

A slave's life hangs in the balance

Onesimus was a runaway slave, a hunted fugitive whose life was in constant danger. He had two options. He could spend his days hiding in the dark, grimy alleys of a Roman city, dodging soldiers and bounty-hunters. Or, he could do the unthinkable and return to his master.

The laws of the empire were harsh. If Onesimus did return, his master Philemon had the legal power to sentence him to immediate execution. If Philemon mercifully decided to let him live, Onesimus would have the letter *F* (for *Fugitivus*) seared on his forehead with a branding iron, marking him for life.

Paul Defends a Runaway

His conversion to Christ through Paul's ministry greatly complicated the decision of the runaway slave. Onesimus knew he couldn't keep running all his life. He had wronged his legal owner and, painful as it seemed, he needed to make amends.

The apostle Paul, sympathetic to the slave's cause, agreed to use his full influence on Philemon. Onesimus's life hung in the balance. This 468-word letter to the slave owner masterfully brings together Paul's skills of persuasion and diplomacy.

Every phrase in Philemon is crafted to produce the best possible effect. Paul appeals to Philemon's friendship, his status as a Christian leader, his sense of love and compassion. He doesn't outright order Philemon to consent, yet he applies blatant pressure, reminding Philemon that "you owe me your very self" (verse 19). Addressing the letter to Philemon's church (verse 2) increases the pressure, as does Paul's promise of a personal visit (verse 22).

Christianity and Slavery

Slavery existed for 1,800 years after this letter was written, and it took the full moral force of Christianity to ban it from the globe. But the tiny book of Philemon shows that the faith had a profound impact on slavery long before abolition.

Christ can revolutionize any social relationship. Onesimus, a runaway, decided to turn himself in. In Philemon, Paul asks for a second miracle. He pleads with the owner to "welcome him as you would welcome me" (verse 17). Such an attitude, in that culture, was social dynamite.

How to Read Philemon

Obviously, Paul had a close relationship with both the slave Onesimus and his owner Philemon. Some scholars believe that Onesimus first heard about Christ when he shared a jail cell with the apostle (see verses 9-10). As you read Philemon, look for clues into Paul's relationship with each person.

Philemon gives us a model of Christian diplomacy. As you read it, think of awkward social situations you know about: two estranged friends or a parent-child conflict, for example. Notice the kind of persuasion used by Paul, and try to apply it to your own circumstances.

Notes

_____

_____

_____

_____

_____

HEBREWS
INTRODUCTION

Time to Decide
Does it matter what you believe as long as you're sincere?

You can go through much of life deliberately avoiding hard decisions. But sometimes you have no choice; the situation forces you to make a decision. Consider an example from the sport of rock climbing.

Sooner or later, every rock climber faces a dreaded section of slick granite that offers no ledges or cracks to grasp. When you come to such a wall, you can abandon the climb. Or, you can risk a move like "the pendulum."

The Pendulum
The pendulum works the way it sounds: as high above you as you can reach, you fasten a loop with a metal nut and slide the rope through the loop. Then you climb down a few feet, dangle on the end of the rope, and try to swing across the sheer section. It takes nerve. You must lean out against the rope into empty space and, with a well-timed push, vault across the face of the cliff. If your lunge toward a safer spot fails, you swing helplessly back and try again.

After your entire party has swung the pendulum, you pull the rope all the way through the loop. From then on, there's no turning back. You have crossed a section of cliff that requires a rope to swing on and a loop to attach it to. The loop is now out of your reach, and the rope coiled at your feet. There is only one way to go: up.

Worth the Risk?
The author of Hebrews wrote to people who faced just such a climactic, can't-turn-back decision. It involved not a rock climb, but their entire future. Should they stick with the familiar routine of the Jewish religion? After all, it enjoyed Rome's official protection and had traditions going back thousands of years. Or should they take a risk and join the growing body of people who called themselves Christians? Those readers needed some compelling reasons to choose Christianity. At that time new converts were being thrown out of Jewish temples, tossed into jail, and even tortured. Was faith in Christ worth the risk?

The tug of the old and the fear of the new kept many interested people, especially Jews, teetering on the edge of Christianity. And the book of Hebrews seems designed to push such people toward a decisive commitment, in one direction or the other. Point by point, the author shows how Christ improved on the Jewish way. Hebrews is a no-holds-barred argument on why Christianity is *better* (a key word in Hebrews) than Judaism. The new faith is worth any risk.

Drawing on the Old Testament
For the sake of Jewish readers, the author painstakingly cites Old Testament passages, more than 80 times in all. He develops the case for Christ like a lawyer, but with the charged emotions befitting the life-and-death issues involved.

Although Hebrews mainly focuses on the Jewish religion, comparing it to Christianity, the book also speaks to our time. Today people ask, "Are religions all that different? Isn't the most important thing to be sincere?" Hebrews insists there are decisive reasons to choose Christ. The author urges his readers to leap forward to a new experience with God through Jesus.

How to Read Hebrews

Who wrote Hebrews? Did the author have a particular group of readers in mind? Scholars have debated these questions for centuries without reaching agreement. The truth is, no one knows for certain either the author or the intended audience of Hebrews.

Nevertheless, the book does give some information about its first readers. They had heard the gospel through contemporaries of Jesus (2:3), and their conversion had brought on physical persecution (10:32-34). One fact leaps out: their spiritual state greatly distressed the unidentified author. Five times in the book of Hebrews he interrupts a careful line of reasoning to fire off a warning (2:1; 3:7; 5:11; 10:26; 12:25).

Hebrews is actually a commentary on the Old Testament. It examines many Jewish customs and shows how Jesus brought about a "better covenant" to replace many of those laws. (*Covenant* means the same thing as *Testament:* a firm agreement between God and humanity.) Therefore, to fully appreciate Hebrews, you should have some familiarity with such books as Exodus, Leviticus, and Numbers.

To follow the logic in Hebrews, note each use of the word *better.* The author compares Jesus Christ to the angels, to Moses, to the priests Aaron and Melchizedek, and to Abraham.

Notes

_____

_____

_____

_____

_____

JAMES

INTRODUCTION

Words Are Not Enough

You can believe all the right things, yet still be dead wrong

Where there is life, there is motion. Some antelopes, as well as the cheetah, can sprint faster than the legal speed limit for cars. Bighorn sheep, charging one another head-first, collide with such force that the sound echoes like a gunshot through mountain ranges. Canada geese, fanned out across the sky in an orderly *V,* battle winds for 1,000 miles, nonstop, before dropping back to earth.

Sometimes we keep relics of life: an elkhead hanging above a fireplace, a fragile, perfect seashell, an exotic butterfly mounted on a pin. But these are mere mementos: life has gone from them, and with it motion.

A Sure Sign of Life

Authors of the Bible often look to nature for analogies to express spiritual truth. And the book of James, controversial because of its emphasis on "good works," is perhaps best understood through the analogy of motion. In the spiritual realm also, where there's life there will be motion.

When a person becomes a Christian, new life begins, and inevitably that life must express itself through "spiritual motion," or good deeds. In James's words, "What good is it if a man claims to have faith but has no deeds?" (2:14).

Movement does not cause life, but it does invariably follow life. It's a sure sign that life is present. Similarly, genuine faith in Christ should always result in actions that demonstrate the faith.

Does James Contradict Paul?

James is not writing about how to become a Christian, but rather how to act like one. Having all the correct beliefs about God will hardly suffice; even demons believe in God. Real, life-giving faith should produce motion, and James minces no words in describing the specific spiritual actions expected of Christians.

Christian thinkers, notably Martin Luther, have struggled to reconcile the message of James with that of Paul, who so firmly warned against slavish legalism. But Paul never belittled holy living. When he wrote to carousers, such as in his letters to the Corinthians, he railed against immorality as strongly as James.

Evidently, James's readers were not even flirting with legalism. They lived at the other extreme, ignoring those laws God had clearly revealed. James had a simple remedy: "Do not merely listen to the word. . . . Do what it says" (1:22).

Straight to the Point

Unlike the apostle Paul, James was no urbane man of letters. He was a simple, homespun preacher, perturbed at people who were not living right. His letter covers a wide range of topics, applying the Christian faith to specific problems and commanding readers to live out their beliefs.

Be humble! James orders. *Submit to God! Stop sinning!* James is as forthright as an Old Testament prophet; it's hard to miss his point.

Modern readers of James face the same dilemma as the first recipients of this unsettling letter. His words are easy enough to understand, but are we doing what he says? What kind of motion characterizes our spiritual lives? As Luther himself said, "You are saved by faith alone, but if faith is alone it is not faith."

How to Read James

Few New Testament writers achieve the clarity or the "punch" of James. He doesn't spend time expanding subpoints or worrying about literary structure. As a result, the book of James reads like a collection of pithy proverbs. (It's sometimes called the "Proverbs of the New Testament.") In your study, it may help to group the material by subject; James tends to return to themes repeatedly.

As leader of the headquarters church in Jerusalem, James knew how to speak with authority. You don't have to look for hidden meanings in this book. James tells you clearly how you should act, in 54 direct commands. Note that many of these have parallels to Jesus' Sermon on the Mount. As you read, keep in mind the diverse audience he was addressing, which included the rich and the poor. Note his "asides" to specific groups.

Notes

_____

_____

_____

_____

_____

1 PETER

INTRODUCTION

A Word to the Suffering

What to do when trouble comes

A distant, swirling cloud of dust signaled the approach of Turkish death squads. But who could escape? The villages of Armenia sat exposed and defenseless on a rocky plain. Doomed

Christians clung together on the floors of their homes, praying, singing, and shivering with fear.

This scene was repeated often during World War I, and it usually ended in a massacre. The Turkish assault against Armenian Christians was one of history's worst religion-inspired bloodbaths: over one million people died. But, sadly, the Armenian tragedy was but one of many attacks against 20th-century Christians.

More people have died for their religious faith in this century than in all the rest of history combined. Thousands of Christians died in East Africa, first in the Mau Mau uprising and then during Idi Amin's reign of terror. Millions more suffered under Soviet and Chinese governments. And the oppression goes on: even today some countries imprison and torture converts to Christianity. This fact alone makes the book of 1 Peter starkly relevant for modern readers.

How to Respond to Persecution

What advice would you give Christians about to undergo persecution? The apostle Peter took up that challenge just as ominous rumblings from Rome were striking fear in every Christian community. Half-crazed Nero had seized on believers as scapegoats for the ills of his empire.

Should the persecuted Christians flee or resist? Should they tone down their outward signs of faith? Give up? Peter's readers, their lives in danger, needed clear advice on suffering.

They also wanted explanations of the meaning of suffering. Why does God allow it? Can good result? Does God care? In short, they were asking the questions that occur to any Christian who goes through great trial.

According to Peter, suffering should not catch a Christian off guard. We are "strangers" (1:17) in a hostile world, and where Christians thrive, storm clouds may gather. Suffering is an expected part of a life of sincere faith.

Peter's Own Experience

On the subject of suffering, Peter makes an ideal counselor, for readers then and now. He had been flogged and imprisoned for his own faith, once even expecting execution (Acts 12). Also, Peter had personally watched Jesus endure suffering, and in this letter he points to him as an example of how to respond.

Peter encourages his readers to "live such good lives among the pagans that, though they accuse you of doing wrong, they may see your good deeds and glorify God" (2:12). Suffering can refine believers and give us an opportunity to prove our faith, the result thus working out for our benefit.

This book emphasizes a further point also: suffering is temporary, to be endured only for "a little while" (1:6; 5:10). Those who suffer with Christ will also glory with him in a life forever free of pain. Skeptics have criticized the church for stressing a future life rather than working to improve this one. "You promise pie in the sky by and by," they taunt. But to Peter's readers—wary of enemies on the prowl, unsure of surviving another day—that message was as tangible and nourishing as food.

According to 1 Peter, our hope that suffering will one day cease is not a mirage but a "living hope" (1:3) in the One who has conquered death.

How to Read 1 Peter

At first Christianity enjoyed official toleration by the Roman empire, but gradually the government turned against it. Rome resented the Christians' talk about another kingdom and their objections to idolatry and decadence.

Although 1 Peter was originally written to people in severe danger, its lessons apply to all of us, for we all experience pain of some kind. Why don't things work out the way we want? Is God trying to tell us something? Peter gives authoritative answers. As you read, try to apply what he says to your own situation.

Peter's writing style reveals his simple fisherman background: he uses pithy peasant expressions and awkwardly shifts back and forth between doctrine and advice. Chapter 2 (verses 18-25) shows an excellent example. Peter gives a deep insight into what it meant for Christ to suffer on our behalf, but he includes it in a practical section on slaves and governments. Thus, he blends doctrine (what to believe) with practice (how to behave).

More a preacher than a writer, Peter structured his book like a rambling sermon. Look for the 34 direct commands included. Peter's reliance on common figures of speech—a cornerstone, a lamb, a shepherd—makes the book very quotable.

But Peter was not simply giving homespun advice; he was well-grounded in the teachings of Jesus and the prophets. Proportionately, he quotes from the Old Testament more than any other New Testament author.

Notes

_____

_____

_____

_____

_____

2 PETER

INTRODUCTION

A Threat from Within
The worst dangers aren't always well marked

First-century apostles must have felt like pioneers in a mosquito-infested swamp. A pest attacked them. *Slap!* They'd kill it, and instantly another would land. Wherever they went new dangers swarmed up.

One group denied Jesus was God; then another declared him God but not fully man. The apostles denounced legalism, only to encounter free-swingers who assumed "anything goes." Members of one church quit work and huddled together to await Jesus' return; those of another gave up on his returning at all.

Second Peter was written in response to a young church's jumpy tendencies. Whereas 1 Peter centered on fearsome dangers from outside, this letter speaks to dangers from within. False teachers were stirring up dissent, questioning basic doctrines, and leading Christians into immorality.

Warning Signs

In its advice to the various squabbling groups, 2 Peter calls for a return to the true gospel. "I will always remind you of these things," the author says (1:12) and proceeds to go over some basic facts of how Christians should believe and behave. The book doesn't introduce many new insights; rather, it erects a giant warning sign against common pitfalls that endanger the church.

A key word, *knowledge*, echoes throughout this letter: 2 Peter refreshes readers' memories regarding the proper knowledge that makes possible "everything we need for life and godliness" (1:3). The author carefully grounds his knowledge in Old Testament prophets and eyewitness accounts of Jesus' life, not in "cleverly invented stories" (1:16). And he urges his readers to resist dangers by living blamelessly.

The answer to false knowledge, the author bluntly insists, is true knowledge; the answer to immoral living is moral living. As he prepares to die (1:14), the author of 2 Peter gets in one last appeal for truth.

How to Read 2 Peter

Although 1 and 2 Peter claim the same author, they have large differences in style and approach. Second Peter is unrefined in writing style, more shrill, and less gentle than the first letter. (Many scholars question whether the apostle Peter actually wrote the whole letter, but the letter does claim his authorship and shows some signs of his influence.)

Perhaps the difference in audiences explains the two approaches. The Bible views suffering—persecution from outside—as a purifying influence that often results in an even stronger church. Thus 1 Peter has an encouraging and devotional tone. But the real danger to a church comes from the inside, from immoral behavior and false teaching. Second Peter, in strong words, addresses those "inside" dangers.

As you read it, try to put yourself in the place of the original audience. What dangers does the author warn against? Are there parallels today? Chapters 1 and 3 can be universally applied.

Chapter 2 concerns itself more directly with the particular false teachers plaguing the first-century church.

In tone and actual content, 2 Peter resembles the tiny book of Jude. Both deal with the same problems and propose the same solutions.

When reading 2 Peter, look for the key words *knowledge, thinking,* and *reminders.* The author appeals to true knowledge that can correct many of the young church's errors.

Notes

_____

_____

_____

_____

_____

1 JOHN

INTRODUCTION

Words That Get Polluted

A problem with the new generation

Over time, common phrases can be stripped of meaning and applied to something else entirely. Take "born again," for example. First coined by Jesus, this phrase was resurrected in the sixties during the Jesus Movement. Soon it was snatched up as an advertising slogan to describe such things as perfume, a used car, and even a comeback football team.

Christianity has been around so long that people borrow its words for quite different meanings. *Jesus,* the center of our faith, is also a common curse word.

Same Words, Different Meanings

This tendency to pollute language is not new. Even at the close of the first century, words were being twisted and drained of their original meanings. When the apostle John wrote his letters, the Christian faith was perhaps 50 or 60 years old. A generation had grown up in Christian homes, and a distinct subculture was already developing.

Some people were using familiar phrases such as "knowing God," "walk in the light," and "born of God," but with new, distorted meanings. The apostle responded with fire. He knew that a confused, subtle distortion of truth is harder to resist than an outright denial.

In this book, John chooses key words (*light, sin, Christ, love, faith,* etc.), "disinfects" them, and then restores their original meanings. He points back to the truths behind the words. Repeatedly, he begins with the phrase, "If we claim . . . " and proceeds to show what actions must result if we claim to live in the true light and know God.

A Step Further

John wrote his Gospel account of Jesus' life in order to bring readers to a belief in Christ (John 20:31). He directed this letter to people who were already Christians, outlining how that faith should affect a person's life. God is light, he says; so walk in the light. He is spirit; so worship him in the proper spirit. He is love; so demonstrate that love to others.

At times John shows the tender concern of a pastor, calling his readers "my dear children" (2:1) and urging them to "love one another" (3:11). But in other places his stern language hints at why he once wore the nickname "son of thunder."

John was probably the last surviving apostle when he wrote this book. He lived almost to the end of the first century. But he was not too old to fight vigorously against whatever might corrupt the faith that had inspired him for so many years.

How to Read 1 John

First John is constructed like a piece of music. Its author states a few simple themes—light, truth, life, love—then builds variations on them. Relying on simple words and a rhythmic style, John writes in universal terms that apply to any time period.

As you read John, note the pattern. He defines a word, such as *light*, discusses its opposite, *darkness*, and then describes what a life in the light should look like. In every case, he shows God as the source of power in the Christian life.

Notes

_____

_____

_____

_____

_____

2 JOHN

INTRODUCTION

Undesirable Guests

When a "Welcome" sign is inappropriate

Roman roads made first-century travel safer and easier than ever before, but Holiday Inns were still centuries away. Therefore, when teachers of the Christian faith traveled the empire, they relied on local Christians for food and lodging.

Before long, false teachers (such as Gnostics) also hit the circuit, joined by religious racketeers attracted primarily to the free food and lodging. The two letters, 2 John and 3 John, the shortest books in the entire Bible, concern themselves with the mounting problems of hospitality for the "circuit-rider" teachers.

Show Discretion, But Also Love

Heresies had already sprung up in many local churches, and 2 John urges true Christians to use discretion in testing a visitor's message and motive. The author cautions against entertaining visitors who do not teach the truth about Christ.

True to his nickname, the apostle of love repeats his motto, "Love one another," even in this letter of warning. The ancient writer Jerome tells of the frail apostle John, in extreme old age, being carried into his congregation mumbling only, "Love one another." When asked why he talked of nothing else, John replied, "Because it is the Lord's command, and if this only is done, it is enough."

How to Read 2 and 3 John

These two books are best read together, since each gives one side of a problem facing a young church. Try to imagine the setting back then, when Christianity was still new and many teachers came along claiming special insights. Do you see any parallels among Christians today? Look for the specific advice John gave in those circumstances.

Notes

_____

_____

_____

_____

_____

_____

3 JOHN

Guidelines for Hospitality

The same questions crop up in every age, in every place

Taken together, this letter and its companion give a balanced view of proper Christian hospitality. Second John warned against entertaining false teachers. But 3 John praises a man named Gaius for warmly welcoming genuine Christian teachers. His actions had been opposed by Diotrephes, a cantankerous church dictator, who was also gossiping against John.

In a very condensed form, John's two letters deal with heresy and church splits, two problems that have plagued the church in every age, in every place. To defend against those dangers, John urges love and discernment. Believers must know whom to accept and support, and whom to resist.

Notes

_____

_____

_____

_____

_____

JUDE

Watch Out!

Sounding an alarm

If you sign up for a driver's training course, you'll begin with several hours of classroom lectures on "Rules of the Road." The instructor will drill you on the shapes and colors of warning signs—signs that announce danger on the highways.

Driving seems all very academic, until you slide behind the wheel. There, a missed stop sign won't just lower a test score; it could cost you your life. Your instructor, rather than calmly correcting you, will shout, "Look out!"

Jude writes in the style of a teacher who is watching a freight train bear down on his student driver. Bells ring out, crossing gates go down, red lights flash. He admits this kind of letter isn't his preference; he intended a more highminded treatise on salvation (verse 3). But the church was facing mortal dangers, and so Jude dashed off a vehement warning.

Who Were the Troublemakers?

Jude doesn't elaborate on what the troublemakers (verse 4) were teaching—perhaps he didn't want to honor their ideas by discussing them. Their behavior, however, is fair game: he fires away at their hypocrisy, divisiveness, and loose morals. He calls them spies and urges believers to fight for the true faith. At his poetic best, he borrows vivid images from nature to describe these people (12-13).

Short and vigorous, the book of Jude brings to mind a message from a fiery Old Testament prophet. Yet Jude holds out hope for his readers. Sincere believers can keep themselves in God's love, and some wavering souls can still be "snatched from the fire" (21-23). (Even when battling heretics, Jude does not hint at persecuting the offenders—no burnings at the stake here.)

Jude closes with a familiar and joy-filled doxology, the one part of his letter still quoted widely in modern churches.

How to Read Jude

In tone, Jude reads a lot like James and 2 Peter: it is simple, hard-hitting, and stern. In fact, it seems to copy entire sections of 2 Peter.

You can read through Jude in a few minutes, to get the force of his argument. But to truly appreciate his letter, you should reflect on (and look up) his various Old Testament references. Jude supports his arguments with extensive illustrations from history, and he even quotes from two Jewish books not accepted as part of the Bible, *The Assumption of Moses* (verse 9) and *Enoch* (verse 14).

All these citations support Jude's main thrust, which he summarizes eloquently in the last few paragraphs.

Notes

_____

_____

_____

_____

_____

REVELATION

INTRODUCTION

A Book Full of Mysteries
Why Revelation is hard to understand

The Roman Empire had its own version of Alcatraz: a rocky island called Patmos. Prisoners banished to that hard-labor colony usually wasted away and died. In that desolate setting a man named John had a series of visions he wrote down as Revelation, the strangest book in the New Testament.

John probably wrote this book about 60 years after Jesus left the earth. Questions were troubling the church. Was Jesus coming back as he had promised? Where did he go? To do what? Why didn't he return immediately? Revelation addresses those issues.

Writing in Code

No other New Testament book resembles Revelation in style. Yet during its time similar Jewish "apocalyptic" books (books that symbolically picture the ultimate destruction of evil and the triumph of good) flourished. Authors, writing to persecuted Christians anxious about their future, predicted what would take place. Often, they used coded language to protect theselves; for example, they substituted a word like *Babylon* when criticizing Rome, just in case their writings fell into the wrong hands.

The codes in Revelation are effective—so effective that few people today agree on exactly what they mean. Some people think many of the predictions in Revelation have not yet been fulfilled; perhaps John was writing about events that will come to pass in our own generation, they say. A best-selling book, *The Late Great Planet Earth,* interprets Revelation that way.

Others explain Revelation in terms of the first century, concluding that many of the events prophesied in code took place during the Roman Empire. Still others find clues to John's meaning spread out over 2,000 years of church history, or surmise that he employed symbols merely to describe an idealized battle of good and evil.

Two Dangers

Because of all the conflicting theories about Revelation, readers are tempted to respond in one of two ways. Some judge the book so perplexingly weird that they can find no reason to read it at all. How can anyone be sure of its meaning?

Others fall prey to the opposite danger. They pore over Revelation and conclude they have discovered the secret explanation of each obscure detail. To the latter group, it may be humbling to learn that every generation since the first century has come up with different interpretations of the prophecies.

Why Read Revelation?

Why read this strange book? John gives a good clue in the first phrase, which introduces this book as "the revelation of Jesus Christ." Revelation gives a unique picture of Jesus Christ, and the New Testament would be incomplete without it. The Gospels describe Jesus' life on earth from four different viewpoints. The letters discuss the deep significance of the resurrected Christ and what he accomplished. But Revelation shows Jesus Christ from a new perspective: as the mighty ruler of the cosmic forces of good. When John saw him in this exalted state, he fell at Jesus' feet as though dead (1:17).

Although Revelation does not remove the mystery surrounding Jesus' return and the end of the world, it does throw light on those events. It cannot be reduced to a mere timetable of events; it speaks lasting truths to every generation of readers. Revelation tells of Christ's future triumph over all the evil in the universe. This crucial message of final hope was needed by its original readers in the first century and is still needed by us today.

How to Read Revelation

Revelation is probably the most intimidating book in the Bible. It packs in so many symbols and obscure details that most readers find themselves plagued by the sensation that they are missing something.

All new forms of writing seem intimidating at first: for example, consider your very first science fiction book, filled with weird names and unearthly creatures, and governed by its own rules of writing. Science fiction seems very strange until you learn the techniques used by virtually all science fiction writers. Once you understand the form, it makes more sense. The same applies to Revelation. It will likely seem strange at first, because it uses techniques of symbolism and visions not commonly used elsewhere in the New Testament.

It is best to read Revelation one vision at a time, rather than all at once. The seven main visions give a view of similar events from different angles.

1. The church on earth (1-3)
2. The Lamb and the seven seals (4-7)
3. Seven angels with trumpets (8-11)
4. The church persecuted by Satan and the beast (12-14)
5. The seven bowls of God's wrath (15-16)
6. Judgment of Babylon (17-19:10).
7. Final judgment and final victory (19:11 to end).

As you read, look behind the visual symbols for the meaning they point to. Ask yourself, What does this tell me about Christ, about God, about the real meaning of history? Don't try to analyze details at first; just follow the main flow of thought.

Keep in mind also the condition of the persecuted Christians who first received this book. They needed not a precise calendar of future events, but rather a word of encouragement and hope. They needed faith that, no matter how things looked, God was in charge of history and good would ultimately triumph. Revelation provides this hope, for them and for us.

Finally, a good Bible dictionary or commentary will clear up much of the confusion about Revelation.

Notes

_____

_____

_____

_____

_____